Finding Wheels

Finding Wheels

A Curriculum for Nondrivers with Visual Impairments for Gaining Control of Transportation Needs

Anne L. Corn
L. Penny Rosenblum

pro·ed
An International Publisher
8700 Shoal Creek Boulevard
Austin, Texas 78757-6897
800/897-3202 Fax 800/397-7633
Order online at http://www.proedinc.com

pro·ed
An International Publisher

8700 Shoal Creek Boulevard
Austin, Texas 78757-6897
800/897-3202 Fax 800/397-7633
Order online at http://www.proedinc.com

Library of Congress Cataloging-in-Publication Data

Corn, Anne Lesley.
Finding wheels : a curriculum for nondrivers with visual impairments for gaining control of transportation needs / Anne L. Corn, L. Penny Rosenblum.
p. cm.
Includes bibliographical references.
ISBN 0-89079-827-3 (softcover : alk. paper)
1. Blind—Transportation—Study and teaching (Secondary)—United States. 2. Visually handicapped—Transportation—Study and teaching (Secondary)—United States. 3. Blind—Travel—Study and teaching (Secondary)—United States. 4. Visually handicapped—Travel—Study and teaching (Secondary)—United States. I. Rosenblum, L. Penny. II. Title.
HV1598.C63 2000
362.4'183—dc21 99-39483
CIP

Photographs were taken by Carrel Grigsby.

This book is designed in Avant Garde and Goudy.

Production Director: Alan Grimes
Production Coordinator: Dolly Fisk Jackson
Managing Editor: Chris Olson
Art Director: Thomas Barkley
Designer: Jason Crosier
Print Buyer: Alicia Woods
Preproduction Coordinator: Chris Anne Worsham
Staff Copyeditor: Martin Wilson
Publishing Assistant: Jason Morris

Printed in the United States of America

1 2 3 4 5 6 7 8 9 10 03 02 01 00 99

Contents

Foreword

It is my pleasure to offer a few words concerning this exciting and significant curriculum, *Finding Wheels*. The authors bring their personal knowledge about many travel-related issues and some possible solutions into focus. Although according to the authors the curriculum "is not a cookbook of the 'how to's' of nondriving," it certainly places many important issues squarely on the table for discussion. *Finding Wheels* is a creative and multifaceted program with the potential to be of immense assistance to adolescents with visual impairment or blindness.

For nearly 30 years the importance of independent travel has been a primary concern of mine. Sharing information about the program and prerequisite skills necessary to succeed with a Seeing Eye dog, my presentations routinely include the kind of issues raised in the *Finding Wheels* curriculum. Building the foundational skills of independent travel may be greatly assisted through using this innovative and student-oriented curriculum.

Although the *Finding Wheels* curriculum targets adolescents, it could easily support discussions for a variety of audiences. The curriculum highlights several key issues such as rites of passage (i.e., the driver's license), personal feelings and attitudes, and the importance of developing good skills. It also brings into focus issues of personal responsibility and taking control of one's life. Regardless of the cause of the visual impairment or the age of onset, the subject matter can be of immense value.

Separating fact from emotion can be difficult. *Finding Wheels* challenges participants through a discussion format that requires student interaction. Using real examples that relate to planning, responsibility, and judgement, *Finding Wheels* does not shy away from some of these more sensitive stumbling blocks.

The *Finding Wheels* curriculum profiles four individuals with differing views about independent travel and the acceptance of personal responsibility. It does not hesitate to shine a healthy light on the emotional stresses of family, friends, and planning for the future. It also supports the idea of effective social interaction and self-determination. Securing the goal to travel independently, whether traveling by foot, by private vehicle, or by public transportation, is within itself significant. The skills and techniques emphasized within this curriculum provide everyday value to a person with visual impairment. Moving with ease, comfort, and style should not be ignored as secondary benefits along the way.

I concur with the author's suggestion that *Finding Wheels* may become part of (a) an orientation and mobility program; (b) course work in independent living; (c) family discussions between parents and adolescents; or (d) as an alternative to driver's education. Further, I believe that *Finding Wheels* answers a critical need and is a valuable curriculum guide. Although many may find themselves sensitive to the material, they will at the same time be sensitized to the fact that there are options that truly warrant investigation and evaluation. Ultimately, the choice belongs to the individual who makes the decision to be goal oriented.

David A. Loux
The Seeing Eye, Inc.

INTRODUCTION: Why Do Nondrivers Need To Discover Wheels?

We would like to welcome you to *Finding Wheels* and hope that you will find that this curriculum will assist you as you help adolescents gain a better understanding of their transportation options. First, we will explain our rationale for developing *Finding Wheels* and introduce ourselves to you and nondrivers. Next, we will provide you with an overview of how to use *Finding Wheels* with adolescents. The objectives for the curriculum are provided in order to give you an overview of the topics to be covered. This chapter ends with a list of questions adolescents can use as they interview nondrivers.

Finding Wheels is a curriculum that may become part of an orientation and mobility program of instruction, a part of coursework in independent living provided by a teacher of students with visual impairments, or part of family discussions between parents and adolescents. It may be implemented as an alternative to driver's education. The curriculum can be used during a summer program for adolescents with visual impairments or as an after-school club. *Finding Wheels* is appropriate for adolescents in upper middle school, high school, or early adulthood. We advocate a team approach to using *Finding Wheels*. That is, families, teachers of students with visual impairments, orientation and mobility specialists, and so forth can all work together to provide adolescents with opportunities to discover their wheels. The variety of ways *Finding Wheels* can be used and the broad age range it encompasses make this curriculum a versatile tool to be used by a variety of individuals.

Rationale and an Introduction to the Authors

Finding Wheels has its roots in our personal experiences; we are both adults with low vision. Our perspectives on nondriving (or in the case of Dr. Corn, both nondriving and low vision driving) are offered to give you an understanding of why we feel this curriculum is an overdue addition to the field of education for adolescents and young adults with visual impairments.

Because we work with young people who have visual impairments and their parents, we are keenly aware of the challenges adolescents face as they come to terms with who they are. Though all adolescents—with and without disabilities—are striving to learn about themselves and their role in the greater society, adolescents with visual impairments face unique challenges. As we begin the 21st century, we find that the key to independence for the majority of adolescents in the United States and other technological societies is the driver's license. When a visual impairment precludes experiencing and benefiting from this rite of passage, it is inevitable that adolescents will question their identities as nondrivers.

Professionals and parents may gloss over the issue of nondriving and subsequently there are many young adults with visual impairments who find themselves on an uncharted course learning to achieve independent travel. Through the development of *Finding Wheels* we found ourselves doing quite a bit of soul searching and a good deal of reminiscing about our own adolescence. We hope that by sharing our own experiences with you, we can help as you use *Finding Wheels* with the adolescents and young adults with visual impairments in your life. You are welcome to share our stories with adolescents as well.

For your assistance, a glossary is provided in the back of the book, and the works defined there are italicized throughout the text.

Anne Corn's Nondriving and Low Vision Driving Experiences

Growing up in New York City, mass transportation was available and a necessity. By about the fourth grade, I took the city bus to and from school and learned the subway system at about the same time as classmates who did not have *low vision*. I couldn't read signs, and thus visual landmarks, colors of lighting in subway stations, using a *monocular telescope*, and even memorizing the order of stations were cues to help me travel independently. The problems began to arise when friends obtained driver's licenses and

I felt very cheated. Trying to appear unaffected, I joined friends who asked me to go with them for their driving lessons. Issues arose with my parents, who insisted on providing transportation during evenings or in poor weather when mainline services would suffice.

As an adult, I moved out of the city. My frustrations began to mount when I found what appeared at the time to be an insensitive response of a midsized city to its mobility impaired citizens. Through committee work, serving on an urban transportation commission, and learning to advocate for others and myself, I became acutely aware of the need to provide nondrivers with information on how to function independently in a motor vehicle dependent society.

Approximately 10 years ago, a new bioptic telescopic system was invented. Although I was aware of former designs, this new lens afforded me a better system with which to learn to drive. For me, learning the visual and other skills needed to drive took a significantly longer period of time than one would expect with typical vision. However, I am now fortunate to enjoy the freedoms and spontaneity that driving affords. Still, I am aware that driving is not for everyone who can meet the visual requirements established by state regulations. It is a complex task which, if not performed well, can lead to tragic consequences. On the other hand, I strongly encourage any adolescent or young adult who meets their state's visual requirements for low vision driving to look into the possibilities and to make mature and thoughtful decisions about learning to drive.

Through my own experiences I have come to learn how infrequently discussions take place with adolescents and young adults regarding strategies for gaining control over transportation needs and challenges. I hope this curriculum will establish a forthright and honest communication about the impact of nondriving among nondrivers, parents, and professionals.

Penny Rosenblum's Nondriving Experiences

As an adolescent in suburban New Jersey, I quickly learned that transportation options consisted of walking, riding my bike, or getting rides from my father and friends. Ironically, my father owned and operated a driving school, a business he established prior to my birth. My mother was his first student, yet by the time I was a preschooler she had decided driving made her nervous, and so all the driving responsibility fell to my father. To say it was "difficult" to be a teenager coming to terms with my nondriving status at the same time my father *literally* was teaching over half the senior class to drive would be putting it mildly.

My first true awareness that life as a nondriver was going to be a challenge was when I went off to my freshman year of college in St. Augustine, Florida. Though many of my classmates did not have cars, most had driver's licenses and thus a better understanding of the community because they understood concepts that I did not (e.g., complicated intersections). Learning my way around an unfamiliar town where I could not see street signs or numbers on buildings made understanding my own transportation needs all the more difficult. When I look back on my freshman year, I wish that I would have had the services of an *orientation and mobility (O&M) instructor* and that I knew there were optical devices for seeing information at a distance. I did not try a monocular telescope until after college graduation, when I was working as a teacher and was encouraged by the O&M instructor serving my students to experiment with one. I have had one ever since and though I don't use it on a daily basis I always have it with me when traveling in unfamiliar environments.

As an adult, I am very selective about where I live, always striving to find housing that maximizes my independence. I am an avid organizer and planner who constantly is thinking of the most effective and efficient way to meet all my transportation needs. My preferred transportation options include public transit, biking, hiring drivers, and exchanging rides (e.g., letting a driver use my washer and dryer in exchange for transportation to and from the grocery store). My greatest frustrations related to being a nondriver are lack of spontaneity and feeling that I waste a lot of mental energy planning and orchestrating my transportation. I am optimistic that within my lifetime technology will be such that I will have the opportunity to explore low vision driving.

How To Use **Finding Wheels** with Adolescent Nondrivers

Finding Wheels is not a cookbook of the "how to's" of nondriving, rather it is a comprehensive collection of information to help adolescents with visual and other impairments begin to evaluate their identities as they pertain to being a nondriver, their transportation options, and ways they can be successful and efficient as nondrivers. *Finding Wheels* has been developed for adolescents and young adults with visual impairments who may or may not have additional mild disabilities. It is our assumption that the adolescents who are using this curriculum have independent O&M skills including but not limited to orientation, cane technique (when appropriate), telephone skills, use of optical devices (for adolescents with low vision), address sequencing, map reading, and money skills.

Finding Wheels is divided into four sections. Section I introduces four adolescent nondrivers. We hope that adolescent nondrivers will find one or more of these individuals with whom they can identify as they move through the curriculum. We encourage you to refer back to the scenarios of the four nondrivers as you and the adolescents move through *Finding Wheels*. In Section II, adolescents are given an opportunity to get to know themselves as nondrivers. This may be the first time that some adolescents will be consciously thinking of life as a nondriver, whereas for others this section will enable them to solidify ideas and strategies they have been considering. Section III examines the variety of transportation options available to nondrivers and low vision drivers. As adolescents move through this section they will have opportunities to familiarize themselves with community resources on the local level. In Section IV, adolescents will examine ways in which they can maximize their own independence as nondrivers through budgeting, route planning, and so on.

Within each section there are units. Each unit contains learning objectives, an ice breaker called Getting Started, a narrative, and learning activities. At the beginning of each unit learning objectives are offered as a way to focus on what specifically adolescents are to master during the unit. The Getting Started feature refers back to the four travelers introduced in Section I and is designed to stimulate discussion about the topics covered in the unit. The narrative provides you with background information on the topics of the unit and information you will need, especially if you are a driver and grew up expecting to become a driver. You may wish to share this narrative information with the adolescents by reading aloud pertinent parts of the unit, paraphrasing what you have read, asking them open ended questions about the topics of the unit, or adding to their responses with information which you have read. In several places examples are given using short vignettes of individuals not featured in the four scenarios in Section I. We do this to further illustrate that each individual will approach the issues of nondriving from a unique perspective. The approach you take in implementing *Finding Wheels* will depend on both you and the adolescents with whom you are sharing *Finding Wheels*.

Following each unit narrative, a list of activities is presented for each of the learning objectives. These activities are provided as a starting point for individual exploration, discussions with adolescents, interactions with other nondrivers, and as a means for seeking information through community resources. Teachers are encouraged to select those activities that will be most beneficial and that may be incorporated into in-class lesson plans, homework assignments, and field trips. Parents may wish to set aside a specific time of day several times a week to move through *Finding Wheels* with their son or daughter. The activities that we have included are only recommendations and serve as a starting point for you to begin guiding adolescents through the exploration of the topics addressed within the unit. Your school and community may provide unique learning opportunities that relate to your geographical location, the people within your community, or specific services available to people with visual impairments or other disabilities. We hope you will design many unique activities and we encourage you to share those with us for inclusion in future editions of *Finding Wheels*.

Each activity is designated as a Self, Others, or Community activity. Our rationale on these three categories is as follows:

- *Self*. These are activities that adolescents can complete on their own. For example, these activities involve reviewing the scenarios of the four travelers, reviewing their own experiences, and consulting their interviews of nondrivers. For some of these activities adolescents may be asked to develop a table or write a paragraph. Other times they may discuss what they have thought or found with you.
- *Others*. These activities are intended to be done with other people. Examples of these activities include role playing and interviews.
- *Community*. These activities are designed to encourage adolescents to get to know the resources in their own communities through using the telephone, library, and Internet to gather information.

As you and adolescents move through *Finding Wheels* we recommend varying the types of activities adolescents are asked to complete. A balance of Self, Others, and Community activities will provide adolescents with a more thorough experience related to the exploration of nondriving. In your planning, select activities that are pertinent to the adolescents with whom you are using *Finding Wheels*. Not all activities will be meaningful to all adolescents and some activities may need modification for a particular adolescent. These activities are only suggested to help as a starting point. We do not expect that all adolescents will need to do all activities before moving on to the next unit.

You will notice some commonalities in the activities in many of the units. We would like to provide some guidelines and recommendations for these activities.

Role Playing

Role playing provides adolescents with an opportunity to try out several approaches for a situation. For example, adolescents may engage in a role playing in which they solicit information from a business owner about the location of the business. If there are two or more adolescents exploring *Finding Wheels*, one may choose to be the business owner and the other may play herself. The scenario may be repeated several times with the business owner being cooperative in one scenario and less than helpful or even hostile in the next. After each role play you may wish to guide the adolescents through a discussion of what they each said, what they may have done differently, and what were effective strategies.

Some adolescents may be going through *Finding Wheels* without peers. It will be necessary for you to become one of the characters during role playing. Adolescents should have an opportunity to play both roles so that they get a better understanding of the perspective of each individual.

Guidelines for role playing include the following:

- Assign roles prior to the start of the scenario and be sure that each character understands the scenario and who is assigned to each role.
- Have participants complete the entire role play prior to the start of discussion.
- Provide each participant with an opportunity to discuss the role play and the behaviors of each character. What did each character do that was appropriate? What did each character do that was not appropriate? What could characters have done differently?
- Allow participants to try multiple roles so they gain an understanding of different perspectives.

Interviews with Nondrivers

Adolescents are encouraged to interview adult nondrivers as they move through the curriculum. In addition, it is periodically recommended that they interview others (e.g., drivers, law enforcement officers). Though this section focuses on interviewing adult nondrivers, the guidelines for interviewing apply to any individuals interviewed during the use of *Finding Wheels*. We recognize that as adolescents move through *Finding Wheels* it will not be practical to continually interview adult nondrivers. Therefore, in the activities at the end of each unit adolescents are asked to review their interviews with adult nondrivers that may have been done earlier in the curriculum. It is recommended that as you begin *Finding Wheels* you provide adolescents with opportunities to interview a variety of nondrivers. Having the opportunity to interview both efficient and not-so-efficient nondrivers will allow adolescents to have more data to compare as they move through *Finding Wheels*. These interviews should be videotaped, audiotaped, or recorded with written notes. This will enable adolescents to refer back to the interviews as they move through the curriculum.

As adolescents make contact with potential adults and schedule interviews, some thought must be given to safety. We recommend that interviews take place in a public place (e.g., the local library, a restaurant, and the school). Teachers may wish to secure written permission from parents of adolescents prior to having the adolescents conduct interviews.

There are many ways to locate adult nondrivers who can provide insight into their own experiences. Potential avenues for locating adult nondrivers include the following:

- contacting graduates of your local school district's program for adolescents with visual impairments;
- contacting your local Commission for the Blind, Lighthouse for the Blind, Vocational Rehabilitation Agency, and so on, and asking them to assist you in locating potential adults to interview;
- placing requests on relevant listservs on the Internet;
- contacting local consumer groups (e.g., National Federation of the Blind, American Council of the Blind);
- contacting the regional office of the American Foundation for the Blind;
- contacting your state's or a neighboring state's residential school for blind and visually impaired students; and
- contacting organizations interested in a specific eye condition (e.g., National Organization for Albinism and Hypopigmentation [NOAH], Macular Degeneration International, Cataract Kids).

We have compiled a list of potential interview questions adolescents can ask during the interview process. This list is provided later in this chapter. The information from these questions will provide adolescents with material to use within each unit. It may be necessary to spend some time with adolescents working on interviewing skills prior to their conducting the first interview. Many adolescents may have never interviewed another individual. You may wish to review the following:

- *Scheduling the interview*. Adolescents should call, write, or e-mail the adult nondriver and explain why an interview is requested. Together they should agree upon a time and place for the interview and estimate the amount of time that the interview will take. Adolescents should gain permission to videotape, audiotape, or complete written notes during the interview at the time they set up the time and place for the interview.

• *Setting up the room for the interview.* Adolescents should select a quiet location for the interview. The furniture should be comfortable. A table on which to keep the interview questions and a tape recorder if one is being used should be available. If the interview is being videotaped, the camera should be set on a tripod that is angled in such a way to include both the adolescent and adult in the frame. All equipment should be checked and set up prior to the time the interviewee arrives so that the interview can begin promptly.

• *Establishing rapport at the start of the interview.* Adolescents should introduce themselves and tell a little bit about who they are and what they enjoy doing. They should ask the adult nondriver to tell a little bit about himself or herself. Once the two have established a rapport, the adolescent should begin with the questions that he or she has prepared.

• *Gaining permission for recording the interview.* At the start of the interview adolescents should inform the adult nondriver that the interview is being recorded (by tape, video, or writing) and should assure the adult nondriver that the purpose of doing this is to allow them to refer back to what is said as they do a series of activities to learn about nondriving.

• *Asking the questions.* Adolescents should move through the list of questions that they have prepared for the interview. However, if the adult nondriver brings up a relevant topic that is not on the list, adolescents should be encouraged to allow the adult nondriver to address that topic.

• *Sending a thank-you letter.* Adolescents should send a thank-you letter in the reading medium of the individual they have interviewed.

Contacting Local Resources

Several times throughout *Finding Wheels* it is suggested that adolescents contact local resources in the community. Each community will be unique and part of the learning process, because adolescents will be discovering what resources are available to them as nondrivers. Adolescents who know in which community they will be living next (e.g., a town in which they will be attending college) may wish to contact resources in the new community so that they will be better prepared when they arrive.

There are many ways to locate community resources, including the following:

- the telephone directory
- directory assistance
- visiting city hall and obtaining a listing of all local offices
- using the Internet if your community has a Web page
- visiting the local library
- asking parents, friends, guidance counselors, and so on
- contacting the local agencies that serve people who are blind in the community (e.g., Commission for the Blind, Lighthouse for the Blind) or other disability groups (e.g., United Cerebral Palsy Association)
- asking adult nondrivers what resources they have found to be of help
- contacting the local chamber of commerce and obtaining a new resident packet or moving packet (there is often a nominal cost for these packets)

As adolescents interact with individuals at community agencies, businesses, and so on, it is important for them to be clear in communicating what information they are seeking. Adolescents should do the following:

- develop a note taking system for their community contacts (e.g., a notebook, a file in their portable note taking device);
- begin all conversations by stating their name and what information they are seeking;
- thank the individual for his or her help, even if the individual did not provide the requested information;
- ask who the individual recommends calling if unable to provide the requested information; and
- repeat the information back to the individual to ensure that it has been heard accurately.

Questions To Ask When Interviewing Adult Nondrivers

Adolescents should have an opportunity to meet several nondrivers so they are exposed to multiple perspectives and experiences. The following is a list of questions adolescents can use during their interviews with adult nondrivers. In the parentheses you will find the unit number to which the question corresponds. Interviewers should ask that the interviewee say if a question is too personal.

- Can you tell me a little bit about yourself? (Introduction)
- What is the cause of your visual impairment (some may consider this a question that is too personal)? (Unit 1)

- Can you describe your functional vision? (Unit 1)
- What were your reactions when you learned that you could not obtain a driver's license? (Unit 1)
- How have you coped with being a nondriver? (Unit 1)
- Where were you able to travel and allowed to travel when you were an adolescent? (Unit 2)
- Did your family encourage you to travel to new destinations when you were an adolescent? If not, how did you discuss your desire to travel with them? (Unit 2)
- How do you structure your life to meet your transportation needs (e.g., selection of housing, proximity to work)? (Unit 2)
- What strategies do you use to meet your transportation needs (e.g., saving up errands and hiring a driver once a week, selecting businesses to patronize on a bus route)? (Unit 2)
- What do you think are the advantages and disadvantages of personal methods of travel such as walking, riding a bike, and using mopeds (if appropriate)? (Unit 3)
- What methods or strategies do you use to locate businesses when you are traveling in the community via walking or riding a bike? (Unit 3)
- What do you think are the advantages and disadvantages of public methods of travel such as taking the bus or subway? (Unit 4)
- What methods or strategies do you use when you call to solicit information from a public transportation operator (e.g., explain you are visually impaired, always have the address of the destination)? (Unit 4)
- What do you think are the advantages and disadvantages of specialized methods of travel such as paratransit services for people with disabilities or charity rides? (Unit 5)
- What methods or strategies do you use when you call to solicit information from a paratransit operator (e.g., explain you are visually impaired, always have the address of the destination)? (Unit 5)
- What do you think are the advantages and disadvantages of hired methods of travel such as taxis or hired drivers? (Unit 6)
- What methods or strategies do you use when you call to schedule a taxi (e.g., explain you are visually impaired, always have the address of the destination)? (Unit 6)
- What strategies do you use to hire, schedule, direct, and fire drivers? (Unit 6)
- What strategies do you use to ask for and decline rides from family, friends, coworkers, and others? (Unit 6)
- How do you pay for your transportation (e.g., allocate a certain amount of money each month, use reduced fare programs)? (Unit 8)
- Do you use reduced fare programs? (Unit 8)
- Do you use a budget for your transportation? If so, how much per week or month do you allow? (Unit 8)
- Do you use exchanging services to meet your transportation needs? (Unit 8)
- How have you learned about transportation options when you've moved to a new community? (Unit 8)
- What strategies or methods do you use when planning routes (e.g., always call the business to get a landmark, use a map)? (Unit 9)
- How do you develop a personal set of directions and where do you store these during travel (e.g., write them down in phrases, use a tape recorder)? (Unit 9)
- What methods and strategies do you use in sharing directions with others (e.g., I print them out a copy in ink print and make a copy for myself in Braille)? (Unit 9)
- How do you calculate the cost of a trip (e.g., what expenses do you consider, do you figure out the costs based on mileage)? (Unit 9)
- What do you do when waiting for late rides (e.g., read a book, write letters)? (Unit 9)
- Can you share any experiences related to transportation where you have had to be assertive or else have had to solve an unexpected problem? (Unit 9)
- Have you experienced frustrations as a nondriver? Can you tell me about them? (Unit 10)
- What frustrates you about being a nondriver (e.g., lack of spontaneity, having to carry all your belongings for the day with you)? (Unit 10)
- What do you consider to be the social aspects of non-driving (e.g., being in charge of the music on a trip, being the navigator)? (Unit 10)
- What do you consider to be acceptable behavior when traveling in public (e.g., starting conversations with other passengers)? (Unit 10)
- When traveling in public, what do you consider unacceptable behavior of others you observe, (e.g., mannerisms such as rocking)? (Unit 10)

You may begin to recognize that some concepts are repeated throughout *Finding Wheels*. This repetition is done intentionally so that such concepts are placed within each topic that is covered. For example, the concept of reciprocation is repeated several times. It is mentioned within a discussion of setting up routine rides, again when there is a discussion of budgeting for transportation, and yet again in a discussion about relationships between drivers and nondrivers. By Unit 8 it may appear that many concepts are repeated. Please continue through all units. This will ensure coverage of all topics and the concepts that are contained within them.

List of Unit Objectives

Unit 1

By the end of Unit 1 adolescents will be able to do the following:

1. Name and describe their visual impairment.
2. Describe the functional implications of their visual impairments for travel.
3. Describe their visual needs to others during travel.
4. Identify reasons why persons with and without disabilities do not drive.
5. Share (to the extent to which they are comfortable) experiences and feelings associated with being told they cannot obtain a driver's license.
6. Identify potential personal reactions to nondriving that affect decisions concerning levels of independence and activity.

Unit 2

By the end of Unit 2 adolescents will be able to do the following:

1. Describe the sequence of independent travel for sighted children and adolescents.
2. Describe different rites of passage for adolescents in technologically oriented societies and how they participate in these rites of passage.
3. Identify destinations where they believe they are capable of traveling and share this information with families.
4. Discuss how nondrivers access transportation and how these methods influence their lifestyles.
5. Describe how nondrivers with different lifestyles structure their lives to access transportation.

Unit 3

By the end of Unit 3 adolescents will be able to do the following:

1. Identify the advantages and disadvantages of personal methods of travel.
2. Solicit information from businesses and other individuals regarding the location of businesses, activities, and so on.
3. Describe considerations for nondrivers using personal methods of travel.

Unit 4

By the end of Unit 4 adolescents will be able to do the following:

1. Identify the advantages and disadvantages of public methods of travel.
2. Solicit information from public transit operators regarding transportation scheduling, costs, routes, and so forth.
3. Describe considerations for nondrivers using public methods of travel.

Unit 5

By the end of Unit 5 adolescents will be able to do the following:

1. Identify the advantages and disadvantages of specialized methods of travel.
2. Solicit information from specialized transit operators regarding transportation scheduling, costs, routes, and so forth.
3. Describe considerations for nondrivers using specialized methods of travel.
4. Demonstrate skills in asking for and declining rides.

Unit 6

By the end of Unit 6 adolescents will be able to do the following:

1. Identify the advantages and disadvantages of hired methods of travel.
2. Solicit information from operators and drivers regarding transportation scheduling, costs, routes, and so on.
3. Describe considerations for nondrivers using hired methods of travel.

4. Demonstrate skills in hiring, scheduling, directing, and firing a driver.

Unit 7

By the end of Unit 7 adolescents will be able to do the following:

1. Determine whether they meet the unaided and aided visual requirements of their state (or a state in which low vision driving is permitted) to pursue driving with low vision.
2. Have knowledge of the clinical low vision evaluation that is needed to determine whether they will meet the aided visual requirements of their state (or a state in which low vision driving is permitted) to pursue driving with low vision.
3. Have knowledge of a variety of bioptic telescopic systems (BTS) and how they are used in the process of low vision driving.
4. Have an understanding of the visual skills needed for low vision driving.
5. Understand some of the differences between driving with low vision and driving with typical vision.
6. Understand some of the legal and self-imposed restrictions in driving experienced by low vision drivers.

Unit 8

By the end of Unit 8 adolescents will be able to do the following:

1. List various sources of funding for transportation, including optional reduced fare programs for those with disabilities.
2. List several tasks that may be offered in exchange for rides.
3. Establish a weekly and monthly transportation budget.
4. Evaluate which forms of transportation are most appropriate to purchase in order to meet current and future needs.

Unit 9

By the end of Unit 9 adolescents will be able to do the following:

1. Use different resources to plan a route.
2. Create a set of directions for personal use.
3. Create a set of directions to share with others.
4. Calculate the time, distance, and cost for short and long distance trips.
5. List several activities that may be done while waiting for late rides in different environments.
6. Be assertive and solve problems concerning transportation schedules for arriving at or leaving a destination.

Unit 10

By the end of Unit 10 adolescents will be able to do the following:

1. Identify personal challenges and frustrations associated with nondriving experience by adult nonrivers.
2. Provide a list of ways to reduce the frustrations associated with nondriving.
3. Identify social aspects of being a nondriver experienced by adult nondrivers.
4. Complete a self-evaluation to determine what skills they still must develop to maximize independent travel.
5. Describe acceptable public behaviors while a passenger in transit.

SECTION I

Teens and Young Adults Who Are Finding Wheels

Section I introduces four travelers, each of whom approaches finding wheels from a different perspective. Those using *Finding Wheels* should take some time to get to know these travelers. You may want to read the stories aloud or select an adolescent to introduce or role-play the traveler using the information presented as a monologue. As adolescents move through *Finding Wheels* they can refer back to the scenarios to see how Pablo, Jason, Kisha, and Mary Ann experienced the topic they are exploring.

The questions and activity below should be used after each of the four travelers is introduced.

Reflection Questions for Nondrivers

1. What is (Pablo's, Jason's, Kisha's, or Mary Ann's) attitude toward being a nondriver? How has his or her attitude changed as he or she has gotten older?

2. What methods of travel does (Pablo, Jason, Kisha, or Mary Ann) use? What does he or she like about each? What does he or she dislike?

3. What methods of travel has (Pablo, Jason, Kisha, or Mary Ann) been exposed to, but has not yet used?

4. What is (Pablo's, Jason's, Kisha's, or Mary Ann's) relationship with his or her family? How do they support or hinder his or her independent travel?

5. In what ways do (Pablo's, Jason's, Kisha's, or Mary Ann's) friends get involved in his or her transportation?

After reading each story, set up 10 chairs in a row. On the first chair place a label, "I am not at all like (Pablo, Jason, Kisha, or Mary Ann)." In the last chair place a label, "I am very much like (Pablo, Jason, Kisha, or Mary Ann)." Ask students to think how much they are like or unlike (Pablo, Jason, Kisha, or Mary Ann) in their approach to travel. Ask them to sit in the chair that reflects their feelings and actions.

Ask students if they would like to move toward or away from either end of the line of chairs. Make a record of the chair each adolescent chooses and the direction in which the adolescent wants to move (if any). This activity may be repeated at the end of the curriculum and change may be shared with the adolescents.

PABLO: "GIVE ME THAT TRANSIT PASS AND I'M GOOD TO GO."

My name is Pablo and I am 19 years old. I live in a small city in the Midwest. I graduated from high school a year and a half ago and am starting my third semester at the local community college. I'm thinking about transferring after my fourth semester to one of the state universities to major in engineering. This past summer I worked in an engineer's office doing clerical and messenger work to learn more about the profession. I think engineering would be a good field for me with lots of rewards and a good salary.

I'm blind due to *glaucoma*—that's when there is too much pressure in your eyes. By the time I was 2, I was blind, so I don't remember if I could see when I was a baby. Every couple of years I go to the *ophthalmologist* so he can check to make sure there are no other problems with my eyes.

When I was about 6 years old, I started working with an O&M instructor and learned my way around my block and school. By the time I was in high school I was traveling around downtown and taking the bus on familiar routes. When I first started community college, my O&M instructor oriented me to the campus, and now it seems like a second home to me.

I live at home with my mom, who works as a nurse in a local hospital. I have a younger sister, Angelica, who is 17 and has a car. My brother Gabriel is 15 and can't seem to talk about anything but getting his driver's license when he turns 16. Sometimes all the talk about driving and cars gets to me, but most of the time I just let it go in one ear and out the other.

When I turned 16 I was really upset that I couldn't go get my driver's license like all the other kids in my class. One night I got really mad at Gabriel over something stupid and started yelling my head off about how everyone hated me and treated me like a little kid. I hung out in my room, listening to my music real loud, something my mom forbids us to do because she says it's going to make us deaf and is rude to the other people around who don't want to hear the music. Anyway, for about an hour she let me sit in my room blasting my music and then she came in and we ended up talking for a long time about what was really bugging me. I told her about all the kids at school who were talking about nothing other than getting their licenses, driving, insurance, and earning enough money to buy their own cars. I told her how lonely I felt, being the only junior who wasn't driving in the whole school and how this made me feel like a little kid.

My mom pointed out that I wasn't a little kid because I was very independent in ways that young children were not. For example, she reminded me that I had a job doing yard work for several neighbors and earned my own money that I put in my own bank account, when I didn't spend it on new CDs. She reminded me that in our church I had gone through confirmation, which meant that I was now an adult. Another thing she said was that I took the bus on my own, not just around our town but to a town about 20 miles away to visit my dad. At that time Angelica and Gabriel were too young to take the bus by themselves, so they had to be driven by my mom or else take the bus with me. Having this talk with my mom helped a little. I began to realize that even though I wasn't getting a driver's license, I was doing things that let me be independent and things that were preparing me to live on my own.

My mom and my O&M instructor, Sandra, must have talked about how angry I was over not getting my driver's license, because a few weeks later Sandra said she had someone she really wanted me to meet. When I asked her who it was, she told me that George was a former student of hers who was home from college on spring break. She told me that George couldn't drive and that when he was my age he was pretty angry about not getting a driver's license, but now as an adult he had found a lot of ways to get around.

George arrived at my school during last period and we got to talk. He was a really cool guy—a senior majoring in English. He asked me how I thought he had gotten to my school for our talk and I figured he had gotten a ride from a family member. I couldn't imagine that he and his dog guide, Nacho, walked from town to my school. He told me that he had taken a taxi and that he used taxis a lot to get around. George did a lot of things I had never tried. For example, he told me that several people in his dorm came to him for tutoring in writing and rather than charging them money like other tutors on campus, he exchanged for rides to the grocery store, to do errands, and to get over to his girlfriend's house so she didn't always have to do all the driving. I had never thought about exchanging for rides and thought it was a neat idea. George said there are some things about being a nondriver that really bug him. For example, sometimes he really wants to go to the mall or some place that is too far away to afford a taxi and there is no one available to get a ride from. He has about $200 a month that he uses for taxis and sometimes to pay for gas for people who drive him places, but he says that a lot of times he runs out of money before the month is over. I could relate to that, as my money never goes as far as I want it to either. Meeting George was really important for me. When I asked him about Nacho, he said that having a dog guide gave him a lot more independence than using his cane. He also pointed out that you have to care for the dog and that it is a lot of work to keep up the training. I had never thought about having a dog guide, but one day I think I will look into it more.

I like to think of myself as an independent traveler, because I make the choices about where I am going to go and how I am going to get there. A lot of times I will choose to walk. From my house I can walk to friends' houses around the neighborhood, the video store, the convenience store, and a couple of fast food restaurants. I use my cane when I walk alone. I like to walk, but it does take a long time and a few times I've gotten caught in the rain.

When it comes to traveling outside of my neighborhood, I take the bus to get to most places I need to go. In my city you can buy a monthly transit pass for college students that costs $12. It's a good deal since a one way fare is $1. I have class 5 days a week, and no matter what I do I never can get all my classes scheduled on Tuesday and Thursday like my friend Rick. Instead, I end up with my classes in the morning every day, which in a way is good because then I have the afternoons free to schedule readers and get my studying done. I've gotten to know a lot of the bus drivers and when they see me getting on the bus they know that I'll ask them to call out all the major intersections so I'll know where we are and when my stop is approaching. Sometimes I get a new driver or have to take the bus to a new place and then I have to be sure to tell the driver that I need the names of the intersections called out. When you take *public transportation* you have to ask a lot of questions and I hate to ask questions. Especially when I am going to an unfamiliar location. Like last month, I had to get to the dentist. I have got to be willing to talk to more people!

One day when I was riding the bus this lady started talking to me about being blind. It turned out she was also disabled. She told me she had a mild form of *cerebral palsy* and could not walk long distances. Sometimes she takes the bus when the stop is close to where she is going, but sometimes if there is a lot of walking involved she will take our city's *paratransit* service. I remembered that Sandra had talked to me about paratransit—you know, those little vans that cart disabled people around from place to place. They're not for me. I can't see myself on some van with a bunch of old and disabled people, no way!

Usually 2 nights a week I get together with some guys with whom I formed a band. I play the keyboard and we're starting to sound pretty good. No paying jobs yet, but we've done a couple parties for friends and stuff. Our band meets over at Eddy's house and I'm able to get there on the bus, and then Rick or Marques gives me a ride home when we're done playing. Rick and Marques won't take any money from me for rides, so once in a while I'll buy the band pizza as a way to say thanks for the rides. Sometimes I get a ride from my mom or sister. My sister always makes a big deal out of how much of an inconvenience it is to have to drive her *older* brother around. I know she is just joking around with me, but sometimes her comments really can be hurtful. One time she said, "Pablo, I wish you would get an eye transplant or something so you can get to places in your own car." I guess I must have looked hurt or something because then she apologized and said that she was just joking. I told her it was OK, but really I was hurt. I find that if I give her a couple dollars for gas, she makes fewer comments and I feel less uncomfortable asking her for a ride.

I'm pretty comfortable with my transportation where I live. I guess that's because I've grown up in the same city and know my way around well and have a good group of family and friends. Because I've been thinking about going to a college in another city, I've been giving some thought to transportation there. I figured I would call Sandra and see if she knows an O&M instructor over there who I could hook up with to learn the community. George's exchanging idea was a good one, and I could see me giving keyboard lessons or tutoring people in math in exchange for rides. I'd sure like to be in a community where there are buses and I guess I will need to look into that, too.

The whole idea of moving to some place where I know no one is pretty scary. I'll have to learn a new transportation system—what I can do by walking, what I can do using public transit, and when I will need to hire drivers to get errands done. I'll also have to figure out how I will pay for all this transportation, too. Maybe I can get a job on campus or teach music lessons to professors' kids. The older I get, the more I come to realize that it isn't that big of a deal to not have a car as long as I plan carefully and stay organized.

JASON: "HELL NO! I WON'T GO!"

My name is Jason and I am 18 years old. Six months ago I finished my senior year at Lincoln High School. I got really tired of people asking me, "What colleges are you applying to?" or "What did you get on the SATs?" It's like this—I didn't want to go to college so I didn't study for the SATs and I bombed them, so even if I *did* want to go to college I wouldn't get in. My folks kept telling me, "Jason, there are all these educational opportunities out there. Since you are visually impaired you can get scholarships if your grades are good. Why don't you just apply yourself, son?" Basically the bottom line is I didn't want high school to end. I had my friends, I knew my way around my school, and I had no major desire to leave home and go "out into the world." After all, each month I now get an Supplemental Security Income (SSI) check and my parents let me keep it as long as I put most of it in the bank. OK, I guess you could say I am a bit of a wimp when it comes to going places.

I have *retinolblastoma,* which means I had tumors in my eyes and my eyes were removed, so I have no usable vision. When I was 10 years old I got an O&M instructor who tried to teach me to use a cane. I just didn't want to learn to use a cane or any of that O&M stuff. My friends would help me get around school and my family would help me when we went places. To me using a cane means that you are "blind" and people don't look favorably on "blind" people as far as I'm concerned. It's not that I mind walking places, it is just that there is nowhere I want to walk that I don't have someone to go with, so why should I use a cane which basically is like painting a sign on yourself that says, "BLIND GUY STRAIGHT AHEAD!"

So anyway, much to my unhappiness high school ended, then my friends all left for college. I didn't have a job and I didn't have any real skills because I had always taken "college prep" classes. I had this counselor from our state vocational agency and she kept nagging me until I went to a 10-week program at a rehabilitation center 200 miles from home. Boy was that an experience! First, I was really angry that I was there with all these blind people. The program had all these classes we had to go to like cooking, computers, and O&M. The first time the O&M instructor told me I was going to plan a route and use the subway to get to the mall, I said, "Hell no! I won't go!" and she said, "Well, that's up to you, but don't you think someday you will want to go get a CD or a new pair of jeans?" I explained to her that I could get a friend or my sister to take me and she started with this "well, what if no one is around, what will you do?" stuff. I did my best to ignore her, but she did make me go out there and take some subway and bus lessons, things I sure don't like to do. I mean, buses and subways are great for people who can see all those signs and can read the schedules on walls and maps, but for someone like me, getting all the information and learning the routes is not easy. I just don't see myself living in a place where I'd take buses and subways. They're the types of things you find in cities and I'm more of a country person.

Living in the country as I do now, the main way of getting around is with someone who is sighted doing the driving. My folks are really great in that they'll drive me places, like to the church youth events or to the mall for me to meet my friend Pete. Most of the time when I am doing stuff out in the community it's with my parents, family, or friends of the family, so driving is not an issue. Once when my dad was out of town on business and my mom's car died, I had to take a taxi from the mall to my grandmother's house. I wasn't sure how to know when the taxi arrived at the mall entrance, so I just stood out there and listened for a car to pull up. Eventually, this guy shouted, "Hey, man, you waiting on a cab?" I said "yes" and got in. He said the next time I called for a taxi I should tell the operator that I am blind so that she'll let the driver know to look for me, since I can't look for him. I assured the guy there wouldn't be a next time. Talk about humiliating experiences!

When it comes down to it, I guess there are a couple of reasons I don't like to travel on my own. First, I feel like everyone is staring at me and thinking, "Gee, look at that blind guy, wonder if he'll fall off the subway platform." I use my hearing a lot and have a really good memory, so some people think I'm faking being blind because I'll respond to something because I hear it or remember it is there. Like in the mall, I will smell the food at the snack bar and then I know that I need to turn left to get to the music shop. People tell me I don't look blind so I guess that's a good thing.

Traveling in a city makes me nervous because I think that I am going to get lost. You know, make a wrong turn and end up in the middle of nowhere or on a block with a bunch of gang members hanging out. There just seems to be so many unknowns when you travel on your own, I'd rather go with someone. Living in the same area all my life, everyone knows I'm blind and so if I really want, I can get rides. It's not like I have anything that pressing that I have to get done, so I just would prefer to wait till my family or my friends are going to the same place. I keep trying to make my folks and that vocational rehabilitation counselor understand that I am perfectly happy hanging out at home and going out places with other people. I get where I want to go, eventually.

KISHA: "THE POWER OF MY OWN TWO FEET."

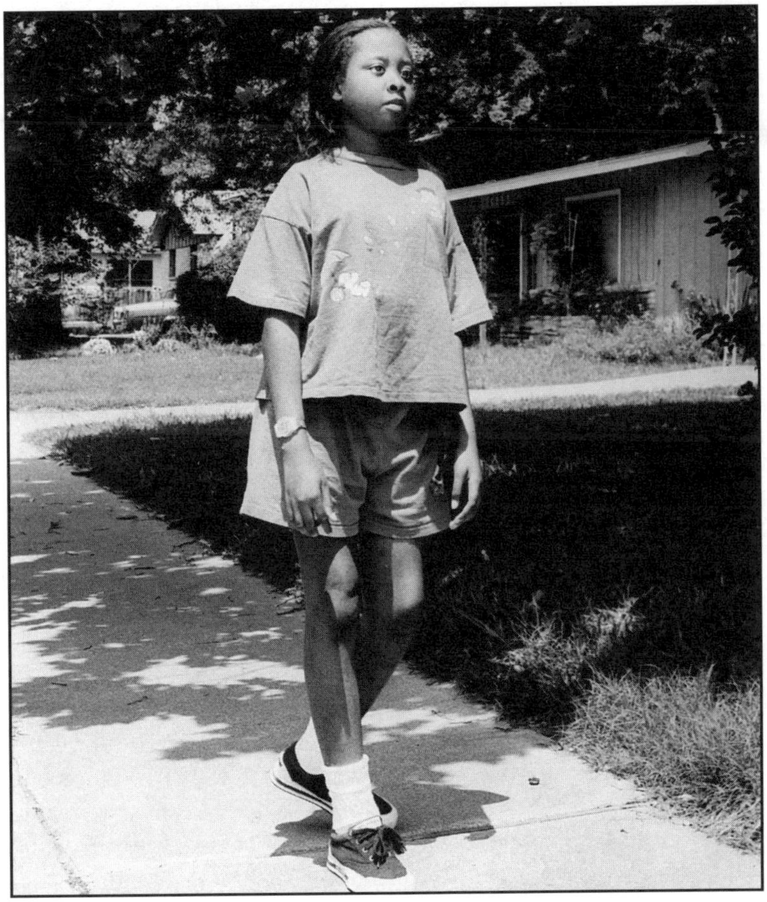

My name is Kisha and I am 16 years old. I was born with something called *cataracts*. That's when the lens inside your eye isn't clear like it's supposed to be, so you can't see real well. I've had some surgeries to try and make things better, but even with the surgeries and my contacts, I still can't see as well as my friends. When I was about a year old my cataracts were taken out. Little babies who are born with cataracts now get them taken out when they are only a couple of weeks old and I've heard that they see better than someone like me who had them taken out when I was a preschooler. We lived in another country until I was 5, where I guess they didn't know about cataract surgery for young kids.

Ever since I was really little I have had teachers work with me who know stuff about how to help you see to read print with special devices. I use a monocular telescope to see the board and the overhead in class. I find that sometimes I can use it for other things, too. Like in assemblies I can see who is up on the stage. One day my friend Ellyn borrowed it to check out the zit on Polly Snoot's nose. After that, Ellyn and I now use my telescope to check out cute guys in the cafeteria. I also have a magnifying glass I use to see little print in books, you know, like textbooks, phone numbers in the telephone directory, and words in the dictionary. When I was 14 my mom and I went to see the *clinical low vision specialist* to see if there were other things that could help me see better. She told us that I could wear special glasses that had little telescopes built into them. She said that with these glasses I might be able to drive, but not in our state. I didn't know, but in lots of states you can drive with special glasses, so maybe when I go to college I'll move to one of the states you can drive in.

Sometimes I have to explain to teachers and other people about what I can and can't see. This is hard for me—I'm really shy and having to take the initiative and say "I can't see the rock specimens" to my science teacher isn't easy. My mom and my teacher for kids with visual impairments keep telling me how important it is for me to speak up for myself and they remind me they won't always be around to lay the groundwork for me when it comes to new situations.

I'm a junior this year and really enjoy doing stuff with my friends—we go to the mall, the park, and hang out at each other's houses. Our town is pretty small, and so I am able to walk to school from my house. I can walk to my friend Ellyn's house, my friend Kathy's house, and my boyfriend David's house. I can also walk to my baby-sitting job that I have every Tuesday and Saturday night at the Connor's. Because it is dark when they get home, Mr. Connor drives me the four blocks home when I am finished working. I also walk to the convenience store by my house to pick up stuff for my family or me.

My mom sometimes gets nervous about my walking around by myself. About 2 years ago we got in a pretty big fight because she didn't want me walking the six blocks to Kathy's house by myself because there is a four-lane road to cross. I told her that Mr. Ross, my O&M instructor, said I could walk on all the streets in our town, except for the highway, which is this six-lane monstrosity. I didn't think my mom believed me so I had her talk to Mr. Ross. He helped her understand that I have learned a lot of special techniques that let me compensate for not being able to see real well. Like, when I go to cross a street, I know I have to really stop and listen for cars along with looking.

We don't have buses in our town, but Mr. Ross has taken me 15 miles down the road to a town where they have buses. He thinks it is important for me to learn all about buses so I can use them if I move to a place where they are available. I'm not real comfortable with the bus thing. You have to read the timetable and map, which I think is confusing. Buses also run on a schedule, which means you're tied to the schedule and if you're running late then you miss the bus. I'm not really an "on-time" kind of person, so I just don't see myself keeping time with a bus. When you walk, you are on your own schedule and that suits me a lot better. When you take buses, sometimes you have to ask the driver if the bus is going to your destination and boy can they be nasty. One guy almost bit my head off when I asked him if the bus was the southbound number 17 bus going to Mission Road. When I told Mr. Ross about that incident he suggested I start my question with a comment such as "I can't see the bus number so can you please tell me if you are the number 17 bus going southbound?" That way the driver will realize I am asking "dumb" questions because I can't see the sign. This seems to me to be a lot of trouble to go through to ride a bus, so I'd rather just walk.

One day Mr. Ross pointed out this van that was in front of the grocery store when we were there for one of my lessons. It said "Dial A Ride" on it and had one of those blue and white disabled signs, you know, like the ones on signs to designate handicapped parking spaces. We watched as an older man with a dog guide got off the van and went into the store. Mr. Ross explained that people with visual impairments and other disabilities along with older people could qualify to ride this service around our town. When we got back to school he *made* me call to get some information about it so I could learn more about who qualifies and how it works. Turns out I would qualify to ride it, but get this—you have to schedule your trips 72 hours in advance. How are you supposed to know what you are going to do 3 days from now?

I'm really a spur of the moment type of person, and without a car that can be a challenge. Like last week, I really wanted to go to the mall to get my hair cut because David had invited me to go with his family for dinner that night to celebrate his sister's engagement. Usually my mom and I go together to get our hair cut, but she was at work so we couldn't go together. I called and the woman there said I could have a 3:00 appointment, but it was already 2:15. If I walked to the mall it would take me at least an hour because it is across town, so I called a taxi to take me there and then I asked my mom to pick me up on her way home. My mom and I agreed that I could have $40 a month for transportation. That's the same amount my friend Ellyn gets from her parents each month for the insurance on her car. Sometimes I use some of my money to put gas in Ellyn's car, some usually goes to taxis, and the rest goes to friends who give me rides to places.

For a while I was getting a ride to and from violin lessons with this girl named Mandy. She was taking piano lessons and so we scheduled our lessons at the same time with different teachers. I would pay her $5 each week for the ride to and from the lesson. Well, one time it was a disaster. Let me tell you what happened. Mandy decided she wasn't going to her piano lesson because she hadn't practiced, but she said she would still give me a ride to and from my lesson. She dropped me off, but then when I was done I waited and waited and waited for her to come back and she just didn't show. I was so bored sitting there waiting, so now I always carry a book to read! When she did come back I asked her why she was 45 minutes late and she told me she was over at the mall hanging out. I told her it was inconsiderate of her to leave me stranded, so I fired her as my driver and found another person who took music lessons to drive me each week. That Mandy sure is rude!

I think that it's good that I live in a town where there are places to walk. I met a girl at summer camp last year who was blind and she lived in the country. There weren't stores or friends' houses she could walk to. I felt kind of sad for her. Walking is important to me and when I pick a college, I am definitely going to try and find one where there are stores and things for me to walk to, and maybe I'll look into driving with those special glasses. Of course, I want a college where they have a good football team and a lot of sororities, too.

MARY ANN: "I'D RATHER NOT BE A BURDEN."

My name is Mary Ann and I am 17 years old and a senior this year. I live in a small town with my dad and two brothers. My mom died when I was 7 and my dad has been raising the three of us with some help from my grandmother. I still miss my mom, even though she has been gone a long time. My dad and I are really close and he looks to me to help with the boys and chores around the house.

I was born really early and I only weighed two pounds, so they had to put me in an incubator. My dad said that for a few days he and my mom didn't think I was going to live. He said I was a real fighter and after 2 months I got to come home. By the time I was 4 months old, my parents learned that I had a visual impairment. It is called *retinopathy of prematurity*. I can see things if they are up close. My brothers get mad at me because I "hog" the television set. I can stand in my backyard and make out that there is a person standing 20 feet or so away, but I can't tell who it is until I get a lot closer. Sometimes my brothers hide from me when I go outside to call them in to do chores before our dad gets home.

As far as schoolwork goes, I try to do as much of it as I can on my laptop computer, which has speech output. My teachers will give me a lot of my assignments on disk and I get most of my textbooks on disk. A long time ago when I was in fifth grade, my dad and I went with my teacher of visually impaired kids to a special clinic where I got a low vision evaluation. There they had all these really cool things—all kinds of magnifiers, telescopes, bioptics, and a *closed circuit television* (CCTV). My school district bought me some equipment, so now I use a CCTV and a monocular telescope. When I was in middle school, a lot of kids would tease me because I had all this equipment and sometimes I'd get really upset because they were picking on me. My dad told me I needed to explain to them that we are all different and each have things we struggle with, and my thing is seeing. Sometimes I would have to explain to the teachers about my equipment and how I needed them to say aloud as they wrote on the chalkboard. It's not easy explaining to people about what you can and can't see, and a lot of times I just let stuff slide. I know it's not a good idea to miss out on seeing stuff because I'm not comfortable telling people about what I need.

I was talking to Ms. Lundy, my teacher for visually impaired kids, and she told me that I am very meek when it comes to speaking up for myself. She told me that I needed to be more assertive about letting people know what my needs are as a visually impaired person. I ended up flunking a biology test because I couldn't see the tags on the samples to know what to identify. I guess she's right—if I don't tell people what I can and can't see, then they won't be aware of the accommodations I need. She also told me I have to become more independent in meeting my transportation needs, but I'm not really sure how to do that.

My brother Derek rides his bike everywhere he wants to go. He even rode it to the mall last week and that is six miles away. My dad says I can't ride my bike in traffic unless I am with someone who can watch out for me, even though I ride my bike around the neighborhood. I was thinking I would ask Derek if I could ride to the mall with him one day. Derek probably would leave me in the dust as we rode, so I guess I won't ask him. Then I'd get lost and never make it to the mall or home again.

I've gone to a summer program for the last 2 years at the school for the blind, which is at the other end of our state, about 300 miles away. It is a cool program. You stay in the dorms and get to take all these classes like computer and drama. The one thing I don't like about it is that you have to take O&M every day. Last year the O&M instructor, Mr. Mende, spent time teaching me about the bus system in the city. We rode the bus together a few times, after I read the schedule to see what time it would come, and I led the way as we walked to the bus stop together. Then he decided I should ride the bus myself, and I wasn't real happy. He told me to meet him at the food court in the mall and that he would buy me a milkshake when I got there. So, I walked to the bus stop and when the bus got there I got on. I couldn't see the number on the front of the bus, but I didn't want to ask the driver like Mr. Mende had told me to do, so I just figured it was the right bus because of the time it got to the stop. Boy was I wrong—it was a totally different bus that went nowhere near the mall! When I realized that, I didn't know what to do, so I just rode it around until it got to the end of the line at the bus terminal. I got off and was going to go find a phone and call the school when Mr. Mende came up to me and asked me what had happened. Can you believe it? He followed the bus in his car when he saw me get on it! I told him I hadn't asked the driver to make sure it was the bus going to the mall. We had a good long talk about my need to be assertive if I am going to be a successful traveler. I just wanted to go back to my room in the dorm and hide after that one!

I have one good friend, Shayla, who is also a senior. She just got her driver's license and she is working at McDonald's almost every day. Her parents are going to help her buy a car. Sometimes they let her borrow their car and she goes to the mall and stuff. Once in a while she will ask me if I want to go, but most of the time she drives over there by herself to meet her boyfriend, Jamal. Sometimes I want to ask her if I can ride along with her, but I don't want to be a burden. I think it really stinks that she gets to drive and I don't. It seems like all the kids at school are going places and doing things and I'm not. For example, I'd like to get involved with the bowling club, but you have to have transportation to the bowling alley. Shayla isn't into bowling and I don't want to ask anyone that I'm not friends with for a ride. I'd really like to go bowling though.

SECTION II

The Realization of Nondriving and Its Implications for Independence as an Adult

Section II contains two units designed to assist adolescents as they explore who they are as individuals with low vision or blindness who will be nondrivers or low vision drivers in the future. In Unit 1, adolescents are encouraged to review their records related to their visual impairment and develop a thorough understanding of how their visual impairment affects their travel. Unit 2 provides adolescents with a chance to explore the concept of rites of passage for both individuals who are sighted and those who have visual impairments. The concept of lifestyle choice is also introduced in Unit 2.

UNIT 1—Understanding Visual Impairment and Its Implications for Nondriving

Understanding how a visual impairment impacts travel begins with understanding medical and functional assessments.

By the end of this unit adolescents will be able to do the following:

1. Name and describe their visual impairment.
2. Describe the functional implications of their visual impairments for travel.
3. Describe their visual needs to others during travel.
4. Identify reasons why persons with and without disabilities do not drive.
5. Share (to the extent to which they are comfortable) experiences and feelings associated with being told they cannot obtain a driver's license.
6. Identify potential personal reactions to nondriving that affect decisions concerning levels of independence and activity.

Getting Started

Remember Mary Ann? She assumed as she was growing up that she would be able to drive a car. It's not that she didn't know she had some trouble seeing. Rather, because all the adults in her life drove cars and because she did not know any adults who were visually impaired, she made the assumption she would drive. After all, she could ride her bike in the neighborhood and walk places. When she started to think about riding her bike to the mall and potentially getting lost, she began to realize that it takes good eyesight to travel outside the neighborhood.

Think About It: Why can't we assume that if someone has enough vision to ride a bicycle, they can safely drive a car?

Introduction

The reality of nondriving can be difficult to accept. Adolescents with very limited or no vision may have accepted that their vision has prevented them from performing certain tasks such as seeing the chalkboard. However, receiving a definitive "no" to the question of driving can force them to revisit issues related to having a visual impairment. The information in this unit will provide an avenue for adolescents to explore their visual abilities and how their visual impairment impacts their travel.

There are several reasons why this unit should come in the beginning of a curriculum for nondrivers. Low vision nondrivers who have a thorough understanding of their visual impairments will be more comfortable communicating with others about why they cannot drive. Also, they will know that it is their decision whether or not to share information with family, friends, and acquaintances during travel experiences, or with people from whom they ask for specific information, such as a bus driver. They will be able to prepare for specific types of visual demands during travel for which optical or nonoptical approaches will be helpful. In addition, this knowledge will help adolescents understand the implications of their visual impairment for not being able to drive and whether they are eligible for services such as reduced fare programs and paratransit.

Debby

Every year Debby went to the ophthalmologist to have her eyes examined and to complete the eligibility paperwork her school required for receiving special services. Following her appointment, Debby and her mother would have a special lunch and attend a play or enjoy the afternoon shopping. One part of the day Debby did not enjoy was when the ophthalmologist would ask her to leave the room so he and her mother could talk. Now that Debby was 15, she decided she was not going to leave the room and would ask the ophthalmologist questions that were on her mind. She wanted to know if her children would have the same condition and if her vision would ever get better. The doctor was pleased to answer her questions and also showed her the form he completed. During lunch her mother said, "I guess we've never asked if you have questions."

Naming and Describing One's Visual Impairment

Although adolescents who are blind should know the etiology of their visual impairment, this section primarily pertains to adolescents who have low vision. Therefore, it may not be as meaningful for those who are blind. Adolescents should have a working knowledge of their ophthalmological and/or optometric reports. This information is important for purposes of eligibility for paratransit services, reduced fare programs, and in some states for the criteria for driving with low vision. They also need a working knowledge of their clinical low vision, functional vision, and, when appropriate, their O&M assessments. Information from these assessments will help them better understand ways in which they are currently using their vision and adaptations that may enhance their visual functioning.

Some students with low vision will use white canes as a travel device or for purposes of alerting motorists to their visual disability. Based on their orientation and mobility assessment, students with low vision will learn if a cane will provide needed information while they travel.

In reviewing their reports adolescents should have a clear understanding of the following:

- *Diagnosis*—the etiology of their visual impairment.
- *Prognosis*—whether their visual condition is stable, improving, or decreasing.
- *Clinical measures*—the components of sight and vision that are measured in a doctor's office; the visual capacity of the person.
- *Visual acuity*—sharpness of detail vision at a specified distance (e.g., 20 feet). The top number (e.g., 20) relates to the distance at which the person can see the object and the bottom number (e.g., 200) relates to the distance at which a person with typical sight can see the same amount of detail.
- *Status with reference to legal blindness*—visual acuity of 20/200 or worse in the better eye with standard correc-

tion (glasses or contact lenses) or a visual field of 20 degrees or less.

- *Visual field*—where the individual is able to see directly ahead, to the sides, and above and below where they are looking.
- *Contrast sensitivity*—the ability to notice the differences between light and dark and between different colors.
- *Color vision*—ability to recognize colors and shades or hues of colors.
- *Light sensitivity (photophobia)*—tolerance for normal levels of light, need for diminished or heightened amounts of light; photophobia refers to a reduced tolerance for light.

There are often misconceptions relating to the status of legal blindness. First, people who are identified as legally blind on a standard (Snellen) eye chart may obtain better visual acuities when presented with a low vision chart that has measures between 20/100 and 20/200. Second, many individuals who are legally blind have good travel vision, even though they meet the legal qualifications for blindness.

Billy

Once Billy's parents learned he was "legally blind," they made certain they were with him whenever he ventured outside. At age 10, Billy had not gone around his corner to mail a letter in a mailbox. However, his visual functioning and orientation skills were such that he was capable of doing so. His vision is actually good enough to apply for a driver's license as a driver with low vision in several states. However, because of lack of experiences and visual skills, Billy may not become an independent traveler.

Describing the Functional Implications of a Visual Impairment for Travel

It is important for adolescents to know how different visual and environmental features impact their use of functional vision. As visual conditions vary, so too does the ability to use vision during travel. Examples of ways in which functional vision is affected include the following:

- *Low contrast sensitivity*—locating curbs, walk lines, seeing colors of lights.
- *Poor acuity*—seeing maps, street signs, identifying small objects in a path, locating and reading addresses.
- *Light sensitivity (photophobia)*—difficulty with sunlight directed toward the traveler, extreme sensitivity to normal levels of outdoor and indoor illumination.
- *Central field restriction*—missing details directly ahead at a distance, needing to turn one's head or eyes.
- *Mid and far peripheral field restrictions*—missing objects to the sides (especially those that are in near space), missing curbs, possible difficulties in low light environments.
- *Poor color vision*—missing objects without contrast to their backgrounds, difficulty identifying objects with color cues.
- *Poor night vision*—having problems with dim light conditions such as dawn, night, or dusk, difficulties with changing lighted environments as when entering a darkened place from a sunlit area.

Some adolescents may have been given *optical devices*, techniques, or other means for reducing these effects or for helping them to cope with various visual challenges. Individuals should know what helps or interferes with their functional vision and which techniques can be implemented. For example, they may be able to read a street sign if they move to a position where the sun illuminates the sign. Some of the conditions that could cause individuals to change techniques, optical devices, or approaches include the following:

- *Changes in flooring levels*—recognizing cracked sidewalks, locating access ramps at ends of blocks.
- *Surface patterns*—discriminating the location of drop offs on floors with complex patterns, recognizing the differences in surfaces (e.g., gravel to grass).
- *Steps*—identifying the top of steps, determining when the bottom has been reached if there is poor contrast.
- *Objects of low contrast*—viewing numbers on elevator panels, finding room numbers in buildings.
- *Shadows*—differentiating between objects and shadows, confusing figure ground in the presence of shadows.
- *Variable lighting within halls and other indoor areas*—avoiding hot spots or irregular lighting created by indoor lights, coping with dim light in unfamiliar environments.

Some individuals with low vision may have difficulty with visual orientation (Ambrose & Corn, 1997). They may have the visual acuity to locate objects, but may not have experiences such as using visual landmarks for orientation. Examples of these difficulties include the following:

- *Misinterpreting objects in the environment*—mistakenly thinking a trash can at 20 feet away is an animal, and not until five feet away realizing it is actually a trash can, or misidentifying a set of stairs as a ramp.
- *Not recognizing where objects or print are located in the environment*—not knowing where to look for addresses on a building or to look for hanging street lights or signs.
- *Not being familiar with signs used for traffic flow*—not knowing that drivers react to green arrows that often come up on traffic lights indicating it is safe to turn left, or not knowing that there are mile posts along the side of the road.

Use of near vision is also important for traveling. Adolescents will need to read maps, time tables, telephone directories, and information presented at their destinations such as receipts, price tags, and bus and train tickets. Use of optical devices may provide adolescents with access to this information. Although some individuals will be efficient users of optical devices for reading school work, they may not have had opportunities to use these devices in the community. Other adolescents will have had only large type available to them in their school and may have the misconception that enlarged print will be available to them in their communities.

Terry

Terry, who had used only large-print texts, was asked how he would determine what time a bus left the mall. His reply was that he would check the bus schedule. When his orientation and mobility instructor handed him a copy of the schedule, Terry said, "I can't read this, I need the large-print copy." His instructor responded, "This isn't available in large type; what are you going to do?" Terry's answer was, "I will give it to my special teacher and ask her to enlarge it for me." The only other option Terry could think of was to ask a bus driver to read it to him, an unrealistic solution. Therefore, it is necessary for nondrivers with low vision to recognize that using optical devices is an option for accessing printed material.

Describing Visual Needs to Others During Travel

Adolescents will have many occasions when they will need to share or choose not to share information about their vision with others. Examples of such situations include asking a classmate for a ride, explaining why they want the bus driver to call out a stop, or responding to a stranger's inquiry about an apparent difference in visual functioning. As independent travelers, adolescents will also be placed in positions where they will need to request assistance. Sometimes they may need to respond to questions posed by others who may or may not be familiar to them. Though this rarely happens for individuals who are blind, those with low vision may find that their visual status may seem vague and raise questions.

When adolescents use optical devices during travel, these devices may increase the number of questions they receive. On occasion, they may result in more offers of assistance. Realizing that a person needs a device to see, a passerby may offer assistance when the device has already provided the access to needed information.

Samantha

Samantha, who is a 17 year old with low vision, has learned that sometimes she has to let people know when she needs assistance. To a classmate she may say, "Bill, I wonder if you can give me a ride home this evening after the game. Even though I can see pretty well during the day, I'd rather not take a bus at night when my vision isn't so good." To a driver she wants to hire Samantha may say, "I have poor peripheral vision. This means I don't see on the sides and may not notice you waiting for me." Finally, to a store clerk who is giving directions to reach the store over the phone she may say, "I will be coming from downtown, can you tell me at what stop I should get off the bus and what is your closest intersection?" In this last instance, Samantha realizes a detailed explanation about her visual impairment is unnecessary.

Identifying Reasons Why Persons With and Without Disabilities Do Not Drive

There are many reasons why people are not able to or choose not to drive. Knowing these reasons, however, may not be comforting to adolescents who are initially coping with their nondriving status. Nonetheless, knowing about these reasons can provide a sense that people do survive without having driving in their lifestyle. Possible reasons for nondriving include the following:

- living in large cities where driving is not necessary because there is good public transportation
- having concerns over the impact of nondriving on the environment
- finding driving to be an anxiety-provoking task
- finding driving to be difficult and complex

- having cultural beliefs (e.g., believing only men should drive)
- having a medical condition (e.g., *seizure disorder*, physical limitation) that precludes driving
- having cognitive deficits that result in difficulty making quick judgments
- lacking financial resources to purchase and maintain a car
- having a license withdrawn or restricted (e.g., drinking and driving)

For those for whom driving is not possible, it is important to understand why society establishes criteria for safe driving. Discussing the criteria for receiving a license (see Unit 7) may help nondrivers come to terms with one of the strongest impacts of a visual impairment—not having the ability to drive in a culture where it is assumed that all adults do so.

Adolescents may not realize that many individuals who do have a driver's license do not have access to a car. Teenagers often cannot afford their own car and are restricted in their use of a family car. College students living in dorms often are not allowed to have cars on campus.

Mary Frances

Mary Frances' Aunt Sophia came to visit from Chicago. Aunt Sophia asked Mary Frances why she was looking so down, and Mary Frances commented, "It's just not fair that everyone but me can drive a car." Aunt Sophia told Mary Frances that she didn't drive a car because driving made her nervous. When she was young her dad had tried to teach her how to drive and then later Uncle Walter had also tried to teach her. She said she found driving to be too stressful and so she moved to Chicago where there were lots of buses and trains, and surprisingly found she loved the city life. Mary Frances still didn't think it was fair that she couldn't drive. In the sparsely populated area where she lived with so few cars, Mary Frances felt she wouldn't hit anything. However, talking to Aunt Sophia helped a little and she realized they had something in common.

Sharing Experiences and Feelings Associated with Being Told One Cannot Obtain a Driver's License

Children and parents often ask professionals about the possibility of driving. Although some medical conditions can change and some children may become more or less efficient using their functional vision, receiving an honest response about driving is very important. If children have clinical measures within their state's regulations for driving with low vision, they should receive information about visual skills that would need to be developed to become a good candidate for a special license.

Many adolescents with low vision ride bicycles independently and therefore believe that they can also operate a motor vehicle independently. For these adolescents, the inability to obtain a driver's license can be extremely frustrating. Many of their friends assume they will be able to drive and explanations become necessary.

Adults who are nondrivers have commented that it is difficult to talk freely with sighted family and friends about their frustrations related to their inability to drive. They worry that significant others who drive might feel that they are wanting pity or asking for more rides. These conversations do need to occur so that significant people in nondrivers' lives can begin to understand the complexities and emotions of nondriving. Adolescents should be encouraged to speak with family and friends about their concerns and together work to maximize independence. Some adolescents will find it helpful to talk about when they learned they would not be able to drive. Others may not yet feel comfortable talking about these memories.

At various times in their lives, individuals will grieve about their disability, and this is a normal reaction. Denial and anger may be exhibited by adolescents; shutting down may be another reaction. It is important for teachers and parents to be sensitive to these feelings and recognize when and if adolescents need to work through the grieving process. Ways to help include the following:

- being an empathetic listener
- providing opportunities for adolescents to talk to adult nondrivers
- providing opportunities for adolescents to talk to a professional such as a guidance counselor or social worker (when appropriate)

Connor

Connor is 15 years old and rides a bicycle to and from school and is an avid skateboarder. On his uncle's farm, he has driven the tractor and the pickup truck. On a recent visit for a clinical low vision evaluation, Connor's father asked the optometrist whether Connor would be able to get a driver's license. Having assumed he would be able to drive, Connor was shocked when the optometrist said he would not meet his state's qualifications for low vision driving. On the way home, Connor's father tried to talk to him about what the doctor had said, but Connor refused to listen. It took a week before Connor would talk to his dad about his feelings of anger and disappointment.

Identifying Potential Personal Reactions to Nondriving That Affect Decisions Concerning Levels of Independence and Activity

Once adolescents have begun to work through feelings related to nondriving, they will begin to make decisions regarding how nondriving will affect their level of independence and activity. At this point, without understanding fully how people who are nondrivers get around, they may inaccurately believe that their activity level will be dependent on other people offering them rides, especially if they live in a suburban or rural area. Coming to believe they can attain independent and active lifestyles is a process that begins with support during this adjustment period. Learning about the range of impact that nondriving can have on their lives is important. Although some nondrivers with many travel needs will consider nondriving a very frustrating and difficult situation, other nondrivers may see it only as a minor inconvenience. For most nondrivers, reactions to living as a nondriver lie somewhere between those two extremes.

LaTisha

LaTisha is 17 and has retinitis pigmentosa (RP), a condition shared by her aunt and her 15-year-old cousin Leroy. Her aunt, who is now blind, has stayed home more over the years and no longer works as an accountant. LaTisha and Leroy both notice the way their aunt has stopped doing many things she used to do. They are determined that if they loose more vision they won't give up things they like to do. They have made a pact that if one says to the other, "I'm not going," that he or she will encourage the other one to get off the couch.

Activities for Nondrivers

Note to teachers: Some families may consider the information in these activities private. Therefore, some adolescents may not wish to discuss their visual conditions. Use discretion in selecting activities for these adolescents and request parent permission for reviewing records with students that coincide with the policies and procedures of your school system.

Activities for Naming and Describing One's Visual Impairments

1. (Self) Ask the adolescents to describe the visual conditions of the four travelers in Section I.
2. (Self) Ask students to review their own ophthalmological, optometric, and clinical low vision reports. Be certain they understand all the terminology and information pertaining to their visual impairment. Provide adolescents with diagrams, books, models, and other materials to facilitate their understanding of their visual impairment and what it means to individual travel.
3. (Self) Ask the adolescents to describe their visual conditions and what is meant by the different terms and numbers on their ophthalmological, optometric, and clinical low vision evaluation reports.
4. (Self) Ask students to develop a list of questions pertaining to their visual impairment that they may ask of their ophthalmologists, optometrists, clinical low vision specialists, parents, and teachers. Possible topics for questions may include which part of the eye is affected, what is the cause of the visual impairment, and what is the prognosis.
5. (Others) Ask students to listen to other adolescents describe their own visual impairments. Ask them to note similarities and differences in clinical measures if both adolescents have low vision (e.g., visual acuity, level of contrast sensitivity).
6. (Others) Ask adolescents to talk to other nondrivers with the same or similar eye condition. They can talk in person, on the phone, or via e-mail.
7. (Community) Ask students to use the Internet, books, or journals to learn more information about their visual impairment.
8. (Community) Ask students to write to organizations that pertain to their visual impairment (e.g., Macular Degeneration International, National Organization for Albinism and Hypopigmentation, RP Foundation). A list of organizations is provided in the resource section in the back of this book.

Activities for Describing the Functional Implications of Visual Impairments for Travel

1. (Self) Ask the adolescents to describe the functional vision of the four travelers in Section I.
2. (Self) Ask students to examine their Individualized Education Programs (IEPs) to see if there are goals to increase visual skills
3. (Self) Ask students to review their functional vision, clinical low vision, and orientation and mobility reports explaining terminology and information pertaining to visual functioning. For those adolescents with low vision, have them give examples of day-to-day experiences to illustrate information in their reports.
4. (Self) For adolescents with low vision, ask them to select five locations they visited in the last week (e.g., mall, supermarket, park, school cafeteria, friend's house). Ask them to describe any problems with environmental factors (e.g., lighting, contrast, locating items, reading prices) that they experienced. Ask them to describe what visual information they used as they traveled there and what information they used when they were at their destination. Discuss any modifications or adaptations used to maximize visual functioning in these environments.
5. (Self) Ask adolescents to identify what their visual needs might be if, for example, they were dropped off at the curb in front of a sports facility or at the edge of the parking lot of a mall.

Activities for Describing Visual Needs to Others During Travel

1. (Self) Review the scenarios of Mary Ann and Kisha, two of the travelers in Section I. Have the adolescents note examples of instances where Mary Ann and Kisha described their visual functioning to others.
2. (Self) Ask adolescents to imagine that they are going to meet a friend in the parking lot of their school after an evening event. What information about their vision, if any, should the friend have?
3. (Others) Review interviews with adult nondrivers for any descriptions of what type of information they share about their vision during travel (e.g., telling a driver they will have a dog guide with them, saying they may not see the driver approach).
4. (Others) Ask adolescents to role-play a variety of scenarios in which one person is a bus driver, clerk, and so on, and the other is blind or has low vision. Provide too much information about the pretend visual impairment and then in another scenario not enough information. Discuss when too much information is not appropriate to get a point across.

Activities for Identifying Reasons Why Persons With and Without Disabilities Do Not Drive

1. (Self) Ask adolescents to make a list of reasons why people may not drive and indicate who they may know in each category.
2. (Others) Ask students to interview individuals who do not drive for reasons other than a visual impairment (e.g., seizure disorders, nervousness, concern over the environment).
3. (Community) Ask students to call the Department of Safety (or the motor vehicle office in your area) to inquire about groups of people who cannot obtain a license or for whom licenses are withdrawn.
4. (Community) Ask the adolescents to call the motor vehicle bureau to gather information about handicapped parking decals (e.g., eligibility, application process).

Activities for Sharing Experiences and Feelings Associated with Being Told One Cannot Obtain a Driver's License

1. (Self) Review the scenarios of the four travelers in Section I. Ask the adolescents to think about which of the four travelers would have been most upset about learning they could not drive.
2. (Self) Ask adolescents to discuss previous interactions with family members and/or eye doctors when they were told they could not drive. Ask them to describe their feelings at that time and how their feelings may have changed over time.
3. (Self) For adolescents who are blind, ask them to recall the time when they understood they would not be able to drive a car. Ask them to discuss if their feelings have changed over time.
4. (Others) Ask the adolescents to write a script of the interaction they had with parents or eye specialists that describes their feelings when they learned they

could not drive. Provide an opportunity for them to develop the script into a group play to be shared with an appropriate audience.

5. (Others) Ask the adolescents to review interviews with adult nondrivers to determine what reactions these individuals had when learning they could not obtain a driver's license. Ask them to compare their own reactions to those of the nondrivers.
6. (Community) Ask the adolescents to locate support groups in the community that address issues for persons with disabilities. Ask them to speak to a member of the group and find out if nondriving issues have been a topic of conversation among the group's members.

Activities for Identifying Potential Personal Reactions to Nondriving That Affect Decisions Concerning Levels of Independence and Activity

1. (Self) Ask the students to review scenarios of the travelers in Section I to see which case most closely represents their own feelings regarding independence and activity?
2. (Self) Ask the students to write a personal statement about how they believe their visual impairment will have an impact on their lifestyle.
3. (Others) Ask the students to review interviews with adult nondrivers to learn about their decisions regarding independence and levels of activity.

UNIT 2— Facilitating Changing Directions: On the Road to Independent Wheels

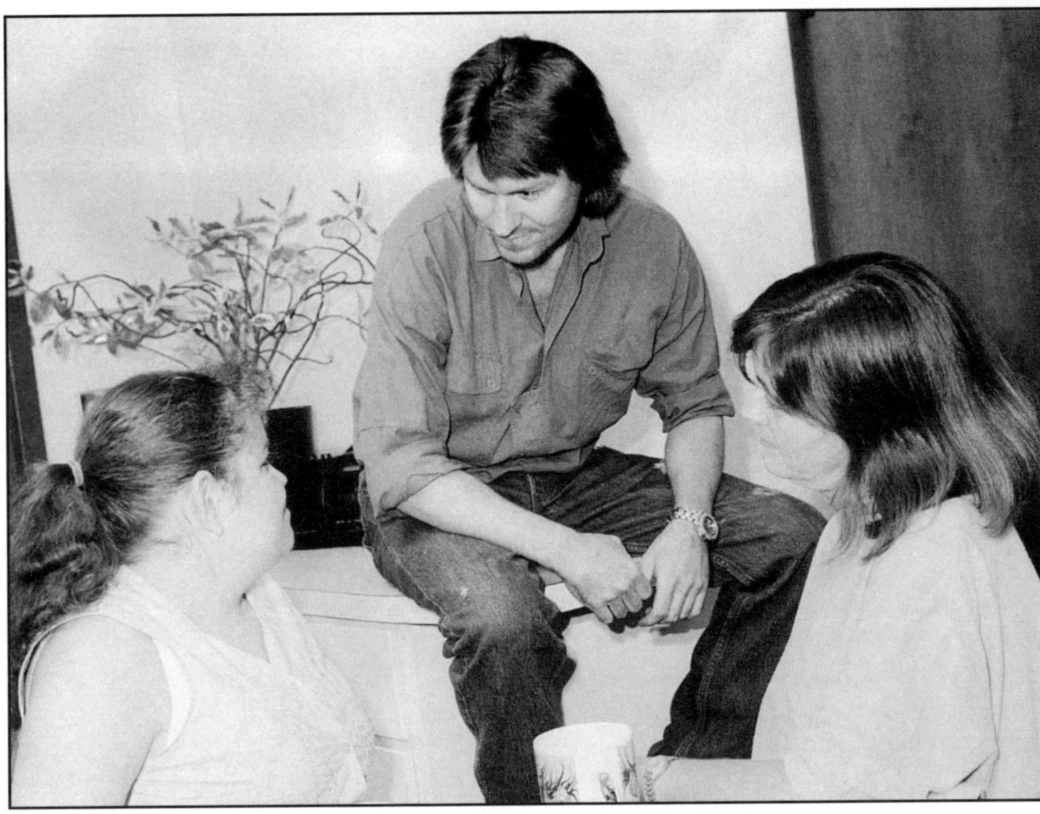

Discussing growing up with a visual impairment enables families to understand an adolescent's responsibilities for meeting their transportation needs.

By the end of this unit adolescents will be able to do the following:

1. Describe the sequence of independent travel for sighted children and adolescents.
2. Describe different rites of passage for adolescents in technologically oriented societies and how they participate in these rites of passage.
3. Identify destinations where they believe they are capable of traveling and share this information with families.
4. Discuss how nondrivers access transportation and how these methods influence their lifestyles.
5. Describe how nondrivers with different lifestyles structure their lives to access transportation.

Getting Started

Remember Pablo and the day he got really angry and had a talk with his mom? He was upset because he felt like he was missing out on a rite of passage—getting a driver's license like Angelica, Gabriel, and other kids at school. After he talked to his mom, he began to realize that there is more to being an adult than driving. Knowing this, however, doesn't always make it easy, because everyone around him talks about cars.

Think About It: How do people know they have "grown up" or "made it" into adulthood?

Introduction

From the first time children venture out of their houses, they are learning about the wonders and the dangers of the outside world. The social experiences of children and their families help to develop travel patterns. Children learn that "going out" may mean taking care of necessities, such as going to medical appointments or to run errands. Going out could also be for pleasurable purposes, such as visiting friends or traveling for the sake of seeing new places. The desire to become a traveler develops as more experiences are provided and as children mature and develop a desire to move out on their own. For sighted children this desire tends to develop naturally. They are able to observe others traveling and are curious about the scenery as they travel to new places. For children who are blind or who have low vision the opportunity to observe how others enjoy traveling may be limited.

The vast majority of adolescents with visual impairments will seek independence and will welcome opportunities to work with O&M instructors to reach their goals. There are other adolescents who may view these lessons with fear or anxiety. The thought of independent travel is frightening to these students and their lifestyle reflects this fear; they restrict their activities so as not to require much travel.

There are also adolescents with low vision for whom O&M instruction is not provided. They get around their schools quite well and O & M instruction for outdoor travel is not considered. However, many of these adolescents can benefit from the skills an O&M instructor can provide. If not previously done, an O&M assessment will provide adolescents and families with needed information about travel abilities.

When families are protective and do not encourage high levels of activity, they may work against the development of travel skills. Acknowledging that there are risks and complexities involved as adolescents with low vision or blindness learn to travel may help teachers and others to understand families' and adolescents' fears. Getting from place to place and using transportation can be a critical step in establishing one's feelings of normalcy. On a daily basis, one's ability to get about projects an individual's autonomy to self and to others.

When fully sighted peers or sisters and brothers receive drivers' licenses, they arrange transportation to go to school events or to jobs. However, too often professionals hear from teenage adolescents with visual impairments statements like "My mother said she couldn't take me," "No one offered me a ride," or "I'd rather listen to the radio" as reasons to stay at home, not obtain a summer job, or choose not to join after-school activities. Some adolescents may believe that locating and employing transportation is the job of parents, teachers, and others. The desire to go places may diminish or never be sparked. Adolescents with visual impairments are at risk of not becoming fully autonomous from families and teachers and later of charitable providers of services for the disabled.

Although some adolescents who will not drive look forward to the time when their brothers, sisters, and classmates obtain their licenses so they can get rides from people other than their parents, others dread the time when their classmates obtain their driver's licenses and their "wheels." For adolescents with visual impairments, this time can be difficult; it is a reminder of the differences that come with being disabled.

Caitlin

Caitlin is a strong student and is in the top quarter of her junior class at Rider High School. She is a competent user of adaptive technology including a portable note taking device and a computer with speech output. Others find Caitlin to be an upbeat friendly person. As her junior year progressed Caitlin became more withdrawn and moody. She told her teacher of students with visual impairments that her moodiness stemmed from feelings of isolation. She felt this way at lunch time and other times throughout the school day when the talk of friends would turn to cars and driving. Even when she would make a comment, about a friend's car or the hassle of getting parents to change a curfew, she still felt that she wasn't part of the group.

Sequence of Independent Travel for Sighted Children and Adolescents

Depending on whether children live in urban, suburban, or rural environments, they will learn to travel in a generally accepted sequence of dependent to independent travel. This sequence of independent travel includes the following:

- traveling independently throughout their houses, their yards, and possibly to a next door neighbor's home;
- traveling to friends' houses within a few blocks or possibly down a rural road;
- traveling to local stores, libraries, and churches either by walking, riding a bicycle, or taking a city bus; and
- traveling to the mall with friends, to downtown business districts alone or with friends, and traveling to the next town or city.

Adolescents with visual impairments may not have the opportunity to go through this typical travel sequence at the same pace as sighted peers or they may skip some of the milestones. By skipping parts of this sequence, they may not develop skills or the practical knowledge that comes with travel in various environments.

There are many reasons why adolescents with visual impairment may not have obtained the same level of independent travel as their fully sighted age mates, including the following:

- difficulty learning orientation skills
- not being provided with any or sufficient amounts of O&M training
- overprotective families and teachers
- living in communities with limited travel opportunities
- presence of additional disabilities that preclude independent travel
- uncertainty of one's own visual or travel skills

Some adolescents are content with the level of travel they have achieved. Others seem caught between the desire to travel more independently but not having the skills to do so. By the time adolescents graduate from high school they should have had the opportunities to travel independently in a variety of ways. It is important that while adolescents are school age they develop travel skills, because adult services may be limited.

Allen

Eighteen-year-old Allen is blind and a senior in high school. He wanted to go downtown from his suburban home and told his mother he would be back by 6:00 p.m., the family's dinner hour. Allen's mother told him to call when he reached the subway stop and his father would pick him up. Allen said he would be happy to walk the six blocks and not bother his father. His mother insisted because it would be dark and she didn't want him to walk alone. At age 18 Allen was angry at being treated like a little kid. However, after years of similar arguments it wasn't worth it to voice his opinion. He left the house thinking, "Won't my mom ever let me grow up?"

Rites of Passage

Rites of passage into adulthood are intertwined with one's family, community, religious group, and socioeconomic status. In many communities and cultures, having a car, or being able to borrow one, is a rite of passage in adolescents' development of autonomy. However, other rites of passage can also provide autonomy and self-determination. These may include the following:

- participating in a religious ritual (e.g., bar/bat mitzvah, confirmation)
- holding a part-time or summer job
- volunteering at a business or agency helping people
- taking on new family responsibilities (e.g., watching younger siblings)

Adolescents and their families need to recognize these other rites of passage. They need to feel they have passed from childhood to adolescence and are moving toward adulthood.

Catarina

Catarina was eager to have her confirmation ceremony take place at church. In her eyes, this was a way for people to finally see that she wasn't a child anymore. After the ceremony, she was feeling very proud of herself, until she overhead two of her grandmother's friends talking as she waited on the refreshment line. The first said, "Mildred's granddaughter did a good job reading, even though that paper was in her face." The second said, "I feel so sad for Mildred having a granddaughter who is never going to be able to live on her own. She'll always have to live with Mildred's son and daughter-in-law because there is no way for her to get around out here." Catarina decided to straighten out these two uninformed old ladies. She put on her best smile and walked up to them to thank them for coming. She told them, "I'm going to miss seeing the two of you here at church, because I'm moving to Connecticut to attend college. I've already gotten an apartment. I hope you'll come with my grandmother to visit."

Identifying Travel Destinations and Sharing This Information with Families

During adolescence it is not uncommon for parents and their children to disagree on what rights and privileges adolescents should have, for example curfews, how tidy to keep one's bedroom, and so on. Similarly, they may have differences of opinion on where adolescents can travel on their own.

Evaluation of travel skills should be conducted on a routine basis by parents, teachers, and the adolescents themselves, taking into consideration cultural aspects of independent travel and safety issues relevant to the community. Because O&M instruction is considered a "related service" under the *Individuals with Disabilities Education Act (IDEA)*, schools are required to provide services to adolescents whose assessments indicate the need for these services.

Isabel

Isabel is 14 and has been working with Mr. Perez, her O&M instructor, all year on crossing lighted intersections and taking buses in her town. At her IEP meeting, Mr. Perez said that he felt Isabel was safe to walk from her home to the high school rather than continuing to take the bus for disabled students. Isabel's parents were very upset that Mr. Perez had put this idea in their daughter's head, as none of Isabel's older sisters who were fully sighted had walked to the high school without an escort. Isabel felt her parents didn't trust her because of her visual impairment, but her father tried to explain that in their neighborhood he wouldn't want any of his girls walking without a male family member. Her parents had permitted Isabel to receive O&M services because they knew someday she would leave home and need to be independent. They had also dreamed that the family would someday move to a safer area.

Access to Transportation and Its Influence on Lifestyle

For adolescents and adults there is a cyclical relationship between travel and lifestyle; the more transportation is available, the more people are able to go places; the more places one would like to go, the more transportation becomes necessary. When the realization strikes adolescents that driving is not a possibility, they must incorporate this knowledge into efforts for choosing their lifestyle and where they want to live. If these adolescents have visual impairments that will allow them to drive in a different state other than the one in which they live, they may plan move to that state after high school graduation. If they attend a residential school for students with visual impairments in a city with good transportation, they may need to decide whether they will return home to a rural or sparsely populated area after graduation. They must examine all of the implications these decisions will have on their family and lifestyle.

For a majority of adolescents, the implications of not being able to drive may be immediate ("I don't want my stepmother taking me to the basketball game this weekend") rather than far reaching ("Will I want to leave my hometown in order to find a job where there is transportation to get to the job on my own?"). It is important for nondrivers to recognize that they have lifestyle choices and a variety of options available to them now and in the future. Rather than staying at home or waiting for someone else to offer transportation, an active lifestyle is a possible for these adolescents.

Forrest

Forrest is a 19 year old who grew up in a large city. He is a potter who specializes in creating unusual plates. As a potter he can live anywhere that tourists would come to buy his work. He decided that a small town would be a good change for him. Although he was initially concerned about whether he would be able to travel independently as his main means of getting around, he soon learned that he could get to about 90% of the places he needed to go by walking or using a bicycle. Within just a few weeks, Forrest was able to find a retired couple whom he hired to run the remainder of his errands with him; when they were not available, he would hire college students from a junior college in the next community. Of course, he would also accept rides from his new friends and neighbors, reciprocating in a variety of ways.

Although adolescents do not have options regarding the type of communities in which their families live, they do have some options about the activities in which they participate and how they travel to these activities. Many adolescents who have driver's licenses do not have ready access to a car. They may be able to borrow the family car on occasion, but their families may not be able to afford for them to have their own car. Therefore, such adolescents often experience many of the issues that adolescents who are nondrivers experience. The following are ways in which adolescents with and without driver's licenses or access to a car travel to activities:

- walking or biking
- taking public transportation such as a bus or a subway
- getting a ride from another person (a parent, brother or sister, or friend)
- taking a taxi
- taking paratransit services

Many adolescents who are going to be drivers or have recently become drivers anxiously search for part-time jobs so they can save to purchase a car or pay for gas and insurance. This motivation brings many adolescents into the work force after school, on weekends, and during the summer. In concert with discussions with parents, and if expected within their culture for sighted students, adolescents who are nondrivers should also consider part-time employment so they can earn money to pay for transportation. Their transportation expenses may include the following:

- bus, train, or subway fare
- taxi or paratransit fare
- money to pay for gas for a friend or family member
- money to hire a driver

Steve

After graduating from high school, Steve entered a college to become a junior high math teacher. During his first 2 years of college, Steve did not work or volunteer his time. Although his academic work load was high during the year, he could have worked in the summer; however, he did not think he needed to because he collected SSI. During his junior year, Steve was required to spend 10 hours a week working in a seventh grade math class at a local school. He had never had the experience of arranging for transportation to travel to and from a job, nor did he recognize the importance of having to be punctual for his work experience. He was repeatedly late and on several occasions did not come to the school at his appointed time because his roommate was not available to give him a ride. He failed his college class in part because he was not responsible in arranging for transportation. Had Steve had prior experiences related to transportation and employment, he would have understood the importance of being reliable during his time at the junior high school.

Different Lifestyles and Access to Transportation

Many adult nondrivers choose to live in urban environments. When selecting their residences they look carefully at many factors including the following:

- availability of trains, busses, and/or paratransit services
- distances to shopping, employment, and recreation activities
- destinations to which they can travel independently
- destinations to which they will need to recruit drivers, take taxis, or exchange with another person for transportation
- the cost for each mode of transportation
- the convenience and desirability of each mode of transportation
- the amount of time each mode of transportation will take to reach a desired destination

Adolescents should think ahead about their lifestyle priorities. They can use this information when they consider where they want to live in relation to how they want to spend their time and money for transportation.

In rural communities and small towns, adult nondrivers will have fewer public and mass transit options. However, they may have rural transportation services, possibly more human resources such as family and friends, and they may feel more comfortable riding bicycles or walking. Creativity often comes into play in order to travel distances that are too far to walk or bicycle.

Brianna

Brianna lived on the top of a mountain that involved a 3-mile drive when coming or going. Because few people would accept money from her, she decided to buy movie passes to give to friends and coworkers who gave her rides. Some people choose to live in communities in which their families live and consider a lack of access to transportation a small inconvenience. Although Brianna was frustrated at times, she could not imagine living away from her family.

Although most adolescents do not have a clear picture of what lifestyle they will want in the future, it is important for them to begin examining what their options and priorities may be and to establish patterns and levels of activity that they may want to carry into adulthood. Many adolescents may not have day-to-day contact with adults who are nondrivers; therefore, they do not routinely observe how different lifestyles create different transportation challenges and solutions.

Chris

Although Chris came from a large city, he and his wife desired a slower paced lifestyle. Because Chris was not able to drive, he and his wife made choices about the type of community in which they believed he could maintain a comfortable level of self-sufficiency. As an artist, Chris looked for a small town in New England where he could become self-employed and establish a network of friends who could barter with him for transportation. It was important to Chris that he have options for transportation besides traveling with his wife. The town they chose had a Main Street along which he could walk to take his daughter to preschool and obtain day-to-day groceries and other conveniences. For major shopping trips, Chris and his wife traveled together.

Activities for Nondrivers

Sequence of Independent Travel for Sighted Children and Adolescents

1. (Self) Ask the students to review the scenarios of the four travelers in Section I to identify where each traveler is able to go independently.
2. (Self) Develop a chart with the following headings: Place Traveled To, Age When First Traveled Independently, and Method of Travel. Ask students to complete the chart by thinking back to such activities as going out in the backyard alone, going to a neighbor's house, going to school, traveling within the mall to a store while a family member was in another store, and so on. Ask them to add destinations to which they have not yet traveled to the chart.
3. (Others) Ask adolescents to interview siblings or classmates to learn at what age they traveled to different locations on their own.
4. (Others) Ask students to interview an O&M instructor to determine how the sequence for independent travel may differ for a sighted and a visually impaired child.
5. (Others) Let students review interviews with adult nondrivers to see if they described information about their sequence of developing independent travel (e.g., a person who might have mentioned the first time he or she took a bus on his or her own).
6. (Community) During travel in the community, ask adolescents to observe the travel skills of sighted children of various ages.

Rites of Passage

1. (Self) Have students review the scenarios of the four travelers in Section I to identify what rites of passage each traveler experienced.
2. (Self) Discuss what is a rite of passage for children entering adolescence and for those entering adulthood. Students should consider milestones such as independent travel, assuming responsibilities in their homes and communities, religious ceremonies, employment (part-time and summer), and so forth.
3. (Self) Instruct the adolescents to develop a chart with the following headings: Rite of Passage, Age Accomplished, Feelings When Accomplished. Have them complete the chart by thinking back to such rites of passage as spending the night at a friend's house for the first time, staying home alone for the first time, completing a religious ceremony, completing the requirements for a badge in Girl Scouts/Boy Scouts, and so on.
4. (Others) Have students interview siblings or classmates to learn at what age they experienced similar rites of passage.
5. (Others) Have students interview a clergy member, employer, and so on, to learn about how that individual views certain rites of passage and what the individual considers to be important milestones during adolescence and young adulthood.
6. (Others) Ask students to speak with family members (e.g., grandparents, siblings, parents) about the rites of passage in their family and community (e.g., going hunting, going on a religious mission).

Identifying Travel Destinations and Sharing This Information with Families

1. (Self) Ask students to review the scenarios of the travelers in Section I to see which person had disagreements with parents concerning travel to a new location.

2. (Self) Ask adolescents to list what they believe to be the set of destinations to which they will be ready to travel within the next year. Ask them to describe how and why they want to travel to these new destinations and what skills they must develop to prepare for this travel.
3. (Self) Ask the students to develop a plan for the next 3 years that will lead to more independent travel. Ask them to detail what the milestones are between where they are now and how they will obtain the highest level of travel over time.
4. (Others) Ask the students to review interviews with adult nondrivers to find out where they went when they were adolescents, and how they may have communicated with their families to let them extend their number of destinations for independent travel.
5. (Others) Ask students to role-play sharing information with parents and other family members about destinations to which they feel capable of traveling.

Access to Transportation and Its Influence on Lifestyle

1. (Self) Ask adolescents to review the scenarios of the four travelers in Section I, noting what types of transportation each person used. Discuss what other options may be appropriate for each of the travelers.
2. (Self) Ask the students to keep a 1-week transportation diary that includes the type of transportation used, planning for travel (e.g., scheduling ahead for a paratransit ride), the destination of travel, the time of day during which travel occurred, and the amount of travel time taken. Ask students to compare diaries at the end of the week and then discuss similarities and differences.
3. (Others) Ask students to interview classmates who may not have frequent access to a car to learn about the types of transportation they access to meet their needs.
4. (Others) Ask adolescents to review interviews with adult nondrivers to examine the types of transportation they used on a weekly basis.
5. (Others) Ask adolescents to interview adults who have a driver's license but do not own a car (e.g., for financial reasons, environmental reasons). Ask students to compare the similarities and differences of lifestyles and uses of transportation between these adults and the nondrivers with visual impairments they have interviewed.

Different Lifestyles and Access to Transportation

1. (Self) Ask students to review the scenarios of the four travelers from Section I. Based on what they know of each of these individuals, ask them to predict where they see these people living in the next stage of their lives, such as going to college.
2. (Self) During trips in the community, ask students to walk or bike carrying groceries or other necessities from a store to a residence (either one's own or an "imaginary" home, i.e., one picked out prior to doing the shopping). Ask them to discuss what it is like to have to carry parcels for a distance on a regular basis. Ask them to discuss how to adapt this activity (e.g., getting a cart, put a rack on their bike).
3. (Self) Ask students to think about how their family transports groceries. If a car is used, what would a nondriver do differently?
4. (Others) Ask adolescents to review interviews with adult nondrivers to learn about the ways in which they structure their lives to meet their transportation needs.
5. (Others) Ask students to interview an O&M instructor who serves adults in order to ask about some of the transportation concerns adults have based on where they live.
6. (Others) Ask adolescents to review interviews with adult nondrivers. Ask them to use these to develop their personal "ideal" lifestyle, describing the places to go and the methods of travel to use to reach these destinations.
7. (Community) Ask adolescents to obtain copies of local transit routes, maps, and apartment finder guides. They should then select a monthly income and locate housing on transit routes. Ask the students to visit the desired home and walk the distance to the transit stop to experience what this would be like on a regular basis.

SECTION III

Transportation Options for Nondrivers and Low Vision Drivers

Section III is designed to encourage adolescents to explore what transportation options are available for nondrivers and low vision drivers. In Unit 3 methods of personal wheels including walking and biking are examined. Public methods of travel including buses, trains, and subways are explored in Unit 4. The concept of specialized methods of travel including paratransit services and charity services is the topic of Unit 5. In Unit 6 hiring drivers, whether a taxi or an individual, is discussed. The last unit in this section, Unit 7, provides information about low vision driving, an option available in a majority of the United States. In this section adolescents are encouraged to try the different methods of travel and learn about these as potential travel options as they move into adulthood.

UNIT 3—Personal Wheels: Walking And Biking

The challenge of completing personal errands sometimes involves independently finding a new address.

By the end of this unit adolescents will be able to do the following:

1. Identify the advantages and disadvantages of personal methods of travel.
2. Solicit information from businesses and other individuals regarding the location of businesses, activities, and so on.
3. Describe considerations for nondrivers using personal methods of travel.

Getting Started

Remember Kisha who had a baby-sitting job twice a week at the Connor's? She would walk to their house, but then Mr. Connor would take her home because it was dark. Kisha knew she was capable of walking alone, but for safety reasons she allowed Mr. Connor to drive her home. Even if she didn't have a visual impairment, in her neighborhood, it is not wise for a girl to walk alone at 10:00 at night.

Think About It: How do you know when someone is offering a ride as a safety precaution and when the offer is because of your visual disability?

Introduction

Some nondrivers will arrange their lives so they can walk or ride a bicycle to accomplish much of their daily activities and errands, or to travel to specific locations such as their place of employment without depending on another person. These personal choices are based on information such as:

- use of functional vision
- orientation skills
- mobility skills using a cane or dog guide
- amount of energy or effort used for travel
- cost
- other available options for transportation

Walking is a method used by many nondrivers for a variety of activities. Some nondrivers will choose where to live so that they can walk to destinations they need to travel to on a daily or routine basis. Many communities are set up to promote walking and bicycling. If businesses are clustered in a part of the community or situated along a road, then pedestrians can easily walk from business to business to complete their shopping, banking, and other essential activities. However, some small towns have businesses spread out over a wide expanse, making walking or other personal methods of travel unrealistic. When friends and family live within close proximity, it is possible for individuals to walk from house to house to socialize. Nondrivers who find themselves in communities that are accessible by walking are able to incorporate this mode of personal travel into their daily routines.

For those with low vision, there are a variety of bicycles, including two-wheel and also three-wheel bicycles, that can be helpful for errands. Nondrivers with visual impairments must be sure that they are safe bicyclists following the same rules as sighted bicyclists (e.g., traveling with traffic, using hand signals). Many cities have bicycle maps and bicycle lanes available that are helpful to bicyclists in planning the safest and most efficient routes.

There are other methods of personal travel that some nondrivers, especially those with good functional vision, may use on occasion. These include the following:

- scooters
- mopeds
- in-line skates
- skate boards
- horses

There are scattered communities in the United States in which cars are not used due to cultural, religious, or environmental beliefs (e.g., Amish communities). Although we do not know of adults with visual impairments who have chosen to live in these communities as a solution to their transportation needs, these communities are mentioned to help adolescents recognize that not all communities are dependent on cars. Travelers with visual impairments who visit many European cities are surprised to discover the ease of walking within many towns. People with and without disabilities in European countries are much more reliant on walking, bicycling, and mass transit than people in the United States.

Doug

Doug and his brother were walkers and hikers. They loved to venture into the woods near their home. Because Doug was blind, they used a compass that was adapted for people who were unable to see. When they hiked they often tried to figure out ways for Doug to remain oriented in unfamiliar locations. They discussed ongoing research that used global positioning systems. They decided that being blind was not going to be a hindrance to Doug no matter where he walked; they might even choose careers that would let them work on this type of technology.

Advantages and Disadvantages of Personal Methods of Travel

Personal methods of travel have both advantages and disadvantages for nondrivers. Advantages include the following:

- Travelers do not need to rely on others;
- Travelers can come and go spontaneously;
- Travelers incur little or no cost when using personal methods of travel; and
- Travelers may experience health benefits.

There are also disadvantages to personal methods of travel including the following:

- They are more time consuming than other methods;
- They may place travelers at risk for crime when walking in certain areas;
- They may place travelers in adverse weather conditions;
- They may restrict where travelers live in a community; and
- Travelers may become stranded without access to a telephone (e.g., getting a flat tire on a bicycle).

Many people with visual impairments carry cellular phones with them for typical communications, as well as for times when assistance is desired. Cellular phones should be considered an extra safety measure and not a tool on which to rely when one lacks proficient orientation skills.

Gregg

Gregg was tired of late rides, arranging transportation, and having to explain why he needed a ride. Gregg's solution was to move to an area where he could be a more independent traveler. Gregg chose New York City as his new home and quickly found a job. When he started to look for an apartment within walking distance of his new job, he soon realized the high expense of living in a community where walking and subways were a viable transportation option. In the long run, however, Gregg felt it was worth the additional rent to be able to walk to stores, movie theaters, and museums, and not have to hire transportation to get his errands done as he did in his suburban community. He could get to the supermarket without planning for a ride in advance. He also felt that he, like many other city dwellers with and without disabilities, chose common transportation options.

Soliciting Information for Planning a Trip

For individuals walking or biking to a destination, it is essential to obtain accurate information about landmarks that will aid in locating a business or activity. Business owners may not understand that nondrivers are asking for details to aid in locating the business. Because they are typically giving directions to drivers, they may become impatient with nondrivers who want to know such information as whether it is a single or multistory building, its location in the block, the color of the sign, or the location of the entrance. Nondrivers may find it helpful to explain that they will be arriving via foot or bicycle and that they have limited or no vision. This will alert the business owner that more details are being sought for a reason, not simply to be annoying.

When planning a trip nondrivers need to do the following:

- Plan adequate time to ensure that they arrive at their locations on time;
- Allow some leeway for finding the location with incomplete or less than exact directions; and
- Remember that estimates given by business employees about the amount of time it takes to walk to a destination may not be accurate for someone with low vision or blindness.

Guadalupe

Asking for information over the phone was never easy for Guadalupe. She disliked having to use directory assistance, because the operators were impatient and would quickly send her call to the recorded number before she had a chance to ask a second question. She also disliked having to say to someone over the phone that she needed directions because she was blind. One day she called a men's store where she was interested in going to purchase a gift for her dad's birthday. To her surprise the sales clerk had very clear directions, even telling her that the building in which the store was located had an entrance that was ten feet past a driveway. When Guadalupe entered the store, she was greeted by the sales clerk who explained that his father is blind and that he was well trained to give precise directions. If only all sales people could learn to give directions so well!

Considerations When Using Personal Methods of Travel

Bicyclists and scooter users will need to follow the same rules of the road as motor vehicles. Nondrivers must familiarize themselves with these rules and strictly adhere to them. When using a bicycle or scooter, safety can be greatly enhanced through the use of a helmet. Indeed, many states have helmet laws. Use of light colored clothing, additional light sources, or reflectors can increase the visibility of travelers.

For individuals who are blind or visually impaired, safety is a concern when traveling alone. Travelers must be able to cross streets safely, remain oriented to their surroundings, avoid becoming lost, and detect obstacles in the environment. If they become disoriented, they will need skills to reorient during travel. Personal safety is especially a concern when traveling in high-risk areas. People with restricted vision may not realize that someone is following them or traveling parallel to them with the intent of causing bodily harm. Some nondrivers with low vision will need to decide whether to use an optical device in a risky area. Showing vulnerability may be unwise.

The following are suggestions for increasing personal safety:

- carrying a whistle or body alarm when traveling to draw attention in the event of an attack
- choosing routes that are well traveled by others who are on foot, bicycle, or skates
- carrying a cellular phone to make an emergency phone call
- traveling at times of the day when there is more pedestrian or vehicular traffic
- selecting routes that are well traveled by motorists (e.g., main streets rather than side streets)
- carrying extra money in case of an emergency (e.g., a flat tire, bad weather) that necessitates calling a cab or a driver

Travelers will need to plan the most efficient and safest route for travel. Bicyclists may choose to go two extra blocks to avoid riding on a busy road that does not have a bike lane. Walkers may walk an extra distance to cross at an intersection with a traffic light. Planning a route that maximizes time use and safety may involve using a map, soliciting aid, or receiving the services of an O&M instructor. Once routes are established, travelers should continue to consider modifications to maximize the effectiveness of the route.

Individuals using personal methods of travel must give consideration to the time of day and the weather conditions. For those who have difficulty with night vision, it will be important to arrive at the final destination prior to nightfall or have well developed O&M skills that enable them to travel at night safely. O&M instructors who work with people with night blindness should schedule lessons in darkness or simulated conditions. Adolescents with this type of problem should understand how methods for adapting to changing light conditions can be helpful. Weather conditions may make independent travel a challenge. Rain, snow, and sleet cause individuals to get wet during travel. In addition, these weather conditions decrease drivers' control over their vehicles and restrict their visibility, a situation about which nondrivers should be aware. Individuals should not take rides offered by strangers. If assistance is needed, the nondriver should ask the stranger to travel to the nearest phone and call a friend or a taxi.

Stephen

Stephen was planning a long distance bus trip to an exotic pet store in a town 25 miles from his home. He called ahead and said he had poor vision and was unfamiliar with the area. By talking with the owner, he learned that the store was 12 blocks from the bus station and that it was in a strip mall with blue awnings. The store owner said that they were located on a busy street, but that he would not recommend Stephen walk on it because there were no sidewalks and lots of driveways with cars pulling in and out. Stephen realized he had choices. He could walk through the neighborhood behind the commercial area in an area of town people had told him was not safe, or he could walk on the busy street and potentially not be seen by a motorist. His last choice was to decide if he wanted to use additional funds he put in his transportation budget to take a taxi from the bus stop or hire his nephew to drive him directly to the store.

Activities for Nondrivers

Advantages and Disadvantages of Personal Methods of Travel

1. (Self) Ask students to make a list of all the methods of independent travel they can think of. For each method, have them list the advantages and disadvantages.
2. (Self) Using the Internet, magazines, books, and other materials, have adolescents research the benefits for both people and the environment of the use of personal methods of travel.
3. (Others) Ask adolescents to review interviews with adult nondrivers to learn what they believe are the advantages and disadvantages of each method of independent transportation and the extent to which the persons use various modes of independent travel.
4. (Community) Encourage adolescents to contact local community resources (e.g., parks and recreation department, transportation commission) to request safety information, city maps of walking/biking routes, and so forth.

5. (Community) Ask adolescents to attend meetings of local committees or organizations that address pedestrian or bicycle travel (e.g., mayor's advisory board, department of transportation, parks and recreation department) to learn about personal travel in the community and what is being done to make personal travel a viable option for individuals in the community.
6. (Community) Ask students to contact the local government agency (e.g., police, pedestrian council) to learn about rules and regulations for in-line skating within the community.
7. (Community) Provide an opportunity for adolescents to contact the Department of Safety (motor vehicles) to learn about licensing and rules related to owning and operating a moped in the community.
8. (Community) For adolescents who are blind, have them contact various dog guide schools to learn of the advantages and disadvantages of using a dog guide during travel.

Soliciting Information for Planning a Trip

1. (Self) Ask students to role-play calling a variety of businesses and other individuals to request information about the location of their businesses. Ask them to compare how they went about obtaining information and the quality of information received.
2. (Others) Ask adolescents to review interviews with adult nondrivers to learn what methods they use to locate businesses and other activities when traveling independently within the community.
3. (Community) Provide adolescents with a map of the city and have them use phone directories and information from businesses to locate the approximate location of these on their maps. With adolescents who are blind, discuss why it is important for them to have this information, such as providing information to a driver.
4. (Community) Review with adolescents the specific numbering system used in their community and provide opportunities for them to predict where a business would be located based on its address. With adolescents who are blind, discuss why it is important for them to have this information.
5. (Community) Review directions with adolescents to ensure their knowledge of sections of the city or community in which they live and the major roadways and secondary streets that can be used to arrive at a destination.

Considerations When Using Personal Methods of Travel

1. (Self) Have adolescents inventory their personal wardrobes to determine what clothing they have that is and is not appropriate to wear during independent methods of travel.
2. (Self) Ask adolescents to review the scenarios of the four travelers introduced in Section I to see what each one considers in determining when and how to use independent methods of travel.
3. (Self) Ask students to develop an emergency plan for if or when they experience an emergency or become lost while using independent methods of travel.
4. (Others) Ask students to interview a law enforcement officer to learn about pedestrian and bicycle safety issues within the community. Have adolescents ask about the safest and most dangerous parts of the community.
5. (Community) Provide opportunities for adolescents to attend bicycle safety and repair classes.
6. (Community) Ask adolescents to take a self-defense class to learn techniques to be used if accosted during independent travel. Ask adolescents to discuss the merits of independent travel in relation to the actual or perceived risk of criminal activity.
7. (Community) Ask adolescents to call local cellular phone companies to investigate the prices and package options available for cellular phone customers.
8. (Community) Have adolescents research where pay phones are typically located within the community.

UNIT 4—Public Wheels: Buses, Trains, and Subways

Bus travel is one method of independent travel.

By the end of this unit adolescents will be able to do the following:

1. Identify the advantages and disadvantages of public methods of travel.
2. Solicit information from public transit operators regarding transportation scheduling, costs, routes, and so forth.
3. Describe considerations for nondrivers using public methods of travel.

Getting Started

Remember Pablo and how he used a bus to travel in his town and to a town 20 miles away to visit his father? Though he was very comfortable using buses traveling on familiar routes, he did not like traveling to new places on the bus. This was because he did not like asking drivers questions. However, Pablo knew he had to do this if he was going to travel independently.

Think About It: How would you handle taking a bus on a route that is not familiar to you?

Introduction

Mainline transportation is the term most frequently used to describe a city's or town's transportation for its citizens; mainline systems may include buses, light rail, and trains. Since passage of the *Americans with Disabilities Act (ADA)* in 1990, mainline services are required to be accessible to people with disabilities. *Mass transportation* usually refers to methods of "people moving" in large cities to reduce heavy congestion on roadways and to encourage people not to use their cars. Intercity buses, Amtrak trains, and planes are forms of mass transportation that are used to travel long distances at a fast speed.

Public transportation carries many people at one time and is available for people who:

- cannot afford cars
- choose not to drive
- are nondrivers who may be disabled or elderly
- are dangerous as drivers

Public transportation may also take the form of rural transit systems that use vans, shared rides, and so forth. They may be more personalized and have some of the features of specialized methods of transportation (see Unit 5).

Skills needed to ride public transportation and mass transportation include the following:

- identifying where passengers are picked up and delivered for outgoing and return trips
- traveling to the point where passengers are picked up
- having the fare available, sometimes requiring exact change
- knowing how to give the fare or obtain a ticket or token for travel and receiving any change owed to the passenger
- obtaining a seat on the conveyance
- having social skills that are appropriate for passengers on the conveyance
- communicating needs associated with identifying stops and disembarking from the conveyance
- understanding what to do, or how to obtain help, should a change occur with the schedule, route, or expected functions of the conveyance, or to facilitate efficiency during transit
- transferring from one bus, train, or plane to another during transit
- locating and traveling to a destination after exiting the conveyance

Eva

Buses, trains, and subways always fascinated Eva, who has low vision. She figured they were there to help people see the entire country, not just for running errands and getting around the city in which she lived. Eva decided to learn to use them very well, because when she graduated from high school she wanted to take a trip all the way to the ocean. Now that's traveling!

Advantages and Disadvantages of Public Methods of Travel

The following are several advantages of using public and mass transit services:

- being able to travel along with others in society (e.g., the feeling of belonging when one is "just another person" riding the train to work)
- having a predictable schedule
- arriving on time or close to on time
- having to pay fares that are lower than the costs of hiring a driver or using a taxi
- not needing to reciprocate or exchange services for rides
- having fixed routes so that this information can be used to locate businesses that will be convenient to stop at along the routes

The following are some of the disadvantages of using public and mass transit services:

- having to travel to the bus, train, or subway stop, and then from the drop-off point to the final destination
- traveling in uncomfortable and sometimes unfamiliar situations (e.g., inclement weather, rush hour crowds, unsafe areas, or at night)

- having feelings of discomfort during travel to and from the bus, train, or subway (e.g., muscle fatigue from carrying groceries and other packages)
- having to wait in inclement weather conditions (e.g., rain, snow, sleet)
- feeling frustrated when the bus, train, or subway is not on schedule
- having to interact with strangers during travel
- being part of a crowd
- being limited by the locations served by public transportation
- being limited by the times public transportation is available
- having to take more time for travel than used by those in personal motor vehicles

April

April lives 2½ miles from a grocery store. She can ride her bike to the store in 20 minutes. However, there are no bike lanes and she does not feel safe riding in traffic. She can walk to the store in approximately 45 minutes, but has found that carrying groceries home for this amount of time is tiring and she thinks that a shopping cart on wheels draws attention to her disability in a way with which she is not comfortable. Therefore, she takes the bus home from the store. She must first travel downtown on the Number 18 bus, which takes approximately 10 minutes. She must then wait 20 minutes for the Number 32 bus, which takes approximately 20 minutes to get her to the bus stop nearest her home. She must then walk the three blocks home. Thus, it takes her about 1 hour to travel the distance of 2 miles, a distance that an individual driving a car can cover in approximately 10 minutes. This also prevents her from buying perishable goods such as ice cream. She must find another way!

Soliciting Information from Public Transit Operators

Information about the schedules and routes of public and mass transit can be gathered over the telephone or in person at a main terminal. Many public and mass transit information centers have detailed information about the physical features of the routes. For example, in some cities information agents are able to tell at what corner of the intersection the bus stop is located, if the bus stop is a bench or a pole with a sign, and what businesses are located at the intersection. Individuals using public methods of travel will need to know the specific location of businesses to which they are traveling, so that information agents can use this information to determine what stop is the closest to the business.

Nondrivers may call an information agent to ask a question about a schedule (e.g., at what time does the Route 9 bus that leaves downtown at 4:20 reach the intersection of Jasper Lane and Highway 42?). When asking this type of question, it is not necessary to inform the information agent that the nondriver is visually impaired. At other times, nondrivers may wish to share this information to clarify for the information agent why detailed information is being requested. For example, when asking on which corner of the intersection the bus stop is located, its distance from the intersection, and what objects identify the stop (sign, bench, covered bus stop) it may be helpful to indicate that the nondriver has a visual impairment and is not familiar with the intersection.

Nondrivers using public or mass transit that arrives or departs from a terminal may speak with the information agent in person. Information agents may not recognize that the nondriver is visually impaired and simply point in the direction of the desired bus, train, or plane. Therefore, the traveler must ask to be given verbal directions.

Dakovan

Dakovan has found he must explain to others why he needs more detailed information in order to locate a conveyance. When at the bus terminal, if he simply asks about routes or schedules, the information agent generally hands him a print copy of the schedule that is not accessible for him. At other times the agent may tell him the information is posted on monitors. He has developed a strategy where he explains he is visually impaired and asks the information agent a detailed question such as, "At what time and from what gate does the next George Street bus headed south leave?" This type of question generally gets Dakovan the critical information necessary to locate his next bus. After receiving the information, he repeats the directions to be certain he understands them and has the correct information.

Considerations When Using Public Methods of Travel

Nondrivers who are successful users of mass and public transportation have well-established O&M and communication skills. These skills include but are not limited to the following:

- knowledge of the structures of different environments
- independence in crossing streets

- independence in locating specific addresses
- ability to solicit aid when necessary
- skills in following directions
- skills in problem solving
- ability to self-advocate
- skills in reading and interpreting schedules
- ability to read maps in order to plan and execute travel
- ability to determine which option is the most efficient if more than one is available (e.g., taking two buses or taking one bus and walking 10 blocks)

Individuals with visual impairments using public and mass transit need to interact appropriately with people they will meet during travel. Effective communication with employees of the transportation system is critical to successful travel. For example, when inaccurate information causes inconvenience, the traveler should remain calm and request assistance. People with low vision often comment that because they do not use white canes or dog guides it is easier for drivers to forget their needs (e.g., that they cannot read street signs while in a moving bus).

Interacting in an appropriate manner with other riders is also imperative. Nondrivers must recognize that it is not appropriate to engage in mannerisms or to talk to oneself while in public. Although it is good to be friendly with other passengers, it is not appropriate to share one's last name, address, or other personal information, nor is it appropriate to ask this information from other passengers. During travel, passengers should keep their belongings with them at all times unless an area for luggage and personal belongings is designated. They should ensure that their belongings do not block aisles or other common areas.

When boarding a conveyance, nondrivers may wish to independently locate or ask the driver where an empty seat is located. If the driver is being asked to identify a stop, it is important for the nondriver to sit near the front of the bus so that the driver will more easily remember the request. If seats are assigned on the conveyance and the nondriver is unable to see the numbers, it may be necessary to solicit aid from an employee or other passenger. While on a lengthy ride, it may be appropriate to remind the driver of the need to have a stop called (e.g., "Are we getting near the intersection of Prince and Fifth?"). It is inappropriate and unsafe for a passenger to engage a driver in conversation while on a bus.

Sandy

Sandy's older brother and his family live out in the country, a 30-minute drive from where she lives in a dorm at a school for blind students where she is a senior. While they often come to see her and take her to dinner, she feels that she hasn't shared in putting forth effort for travel. Sandy found out there is a bus she can take from a central location that takes approximately 1 hour and 15 minutes to get to the town where her brother and his family live. In addition, it takes 20 minutes to get to the bus station and she must arrive to pick up her ticket at least 10 minutes before the departure time. It will also take 10 minutes to walk from the bus stop to her brother's home. Altogether, taking public transportation will take 1 hour and 45 minutes, compared to what a driver could do in 30 minutes. Sandy didn't have funds to take a taxi and so she woke up quite early to take this trip. After her visit, her sister-in-law gave her a ride back. This saved Sandy 45 minutes, but then she realized that her sister-in-law had an hour's trip going both ways. Why does public transportation create such problems?

Activities for Nondrivers

Advantages and Disadvantages of Public Methods of Travel

1. (Self) Ask students to review the scenarios of the four travelers introduced in Section I to see what methods of public transportation each used and what advantages and disadvantages the travelers identified.
2. (Self) Ask adolescents to make a list of all the methods of public travel they can think of. For each method, have them list the advantages and disadvantages for the method. This may be written as a public relations brochure or as a sales brochure to increase ridership.
3. (Self) Have adolescents discuss possible differences in the use of public transit for people with and without visual impairments.
4. (Others) Ask students to review interviews with adult nondrivers to learn what they believe are the advantages and disadvantages of each method of public transportation.
5. (Community) Encourage adolescents to contact local community providers of public transit (e.g., public transit authority, bus companies) to request informa-

tion on services for people with disabilities who use public transit (e.g., large print or braille schedules, signage, and visual and tactual maps).

Soliciting Information from Public Transit Operators

1. (Self) Ask adolescents to generate a list of all the possible questions they may need to ask a public transit operator. Then ask them to examine their lists and determine which of the questions are ones that anyone would ask and which are ones specific to people with visual impairments.

2. (Self) Ask students to role-play calling public transit operators to request information about routes and schedules for similar and different destinations.

3. (Self) Have adolescents locate phone numbers of public transit agencies using a phone book and the directory assistance operator. Students who are blind and those who cannot access standard print with optical devices should have a working knowledge of the information and format found in directories. They should direct a reader to read the information needed.

4. (Self) Provide adolescents with maps of the community and have them develop personalized maps showing the routes of public transit they wish to take and the businesses and activities along the routes they wish to visit. Have them use their maps during a trip in the community. For adolescents who are blind, ask them to use a sighted assistant to obtain the information from the map, and to create a tactual map.

5. (Others) Ask adolescents to review interviews with adult nondrivers to learn what methods they use when calling to solicit information from public transit operators.

6. (Others) Ask adolescents to work together to develop an informational session about passengers with visual impairments for bus drivers, train operators, or other personnel in public transit.

7. (Community) Review with adolescents the components of a public transit schedule, having them call the transit operator to ask specific questions about routes, schedules, and accommodations for individuals with disabilities.

Considerations When Using Public Methods of Travel

1. (Self) Ask adolescents to role-play appropriate and inappropriate ways of asking drivers, information agents, and other travelers information (e.g., "Which train is this?" "Can you call out my stop?").

2. (Self) Ask adolescents to develop an emergency plan for if or when they miss a transfer, get off the public method of travel in the wrong location, and so on.

3. (Self) Ask students to develop an information brochure for individuals with visual impairment about what can go wrong and what can go right when using public transit.

4. (Others) Ask adolescents to interview drivers to learn about when they choose to use public methods of travel or why they choose not to consider these options.

UNIT 5—Specialized Wheels: Paratransit, Charity Services, and Volunteer Services

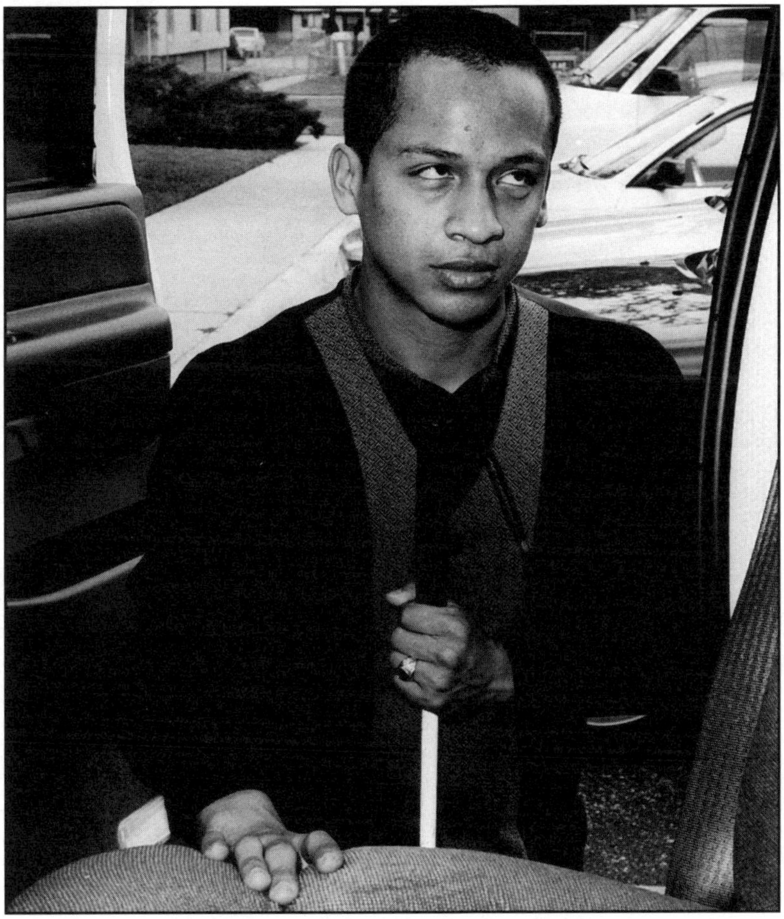

Paratransit vehicles provide door-to-door service for those who are eligible.

By the end of this unit adolescents will be able to do the following:

1. Identify the advantages and disadvantages of specialized methods of travel.
2. Solicit information from specialized transit operators regarding transportation scheduling, costs, routes, and so forth.
3. Describe considerations for nondrivers using specialized methods of travel.
4. Demonstrate skills in asking for and declining rides.

Getting Started

Remember how Jason was happy to let other people drive him places or to stay home if no one was around to take him? Although Jason's parents love him, they will not be around forever to provide rides. His friends will become busier and busier with college and work and Jason may find that his "volunteer" drivers dwindle down to an occasional ride. The little bit of desire Jason does have to go to the mall and to church events may diminish over time, leaving Jason to be a couch potato. Depending exclusively on people to volunteer rides isn't the best route for Jason to go.

Think About It: Rides are often provided out of friendship and love of a family member. How will you react when others believe you are imposing on them? Was Jason able to distinguish between these two types of rides?

Introduction

Specialized services are those designed and provided for persons who cannot drive due to a disability or other reasons as stipulated by the provider of the service. These services cannot be accessed by just any citizen. These services do not require the level of independence that is required of users of public transportation. They provide more personal attention, but they are usually more restrictive in regards to when they are available.

Paratransit services, though specialized, are part of the public transportation system in that they are generally paid for by public funding and riders are required to pay a fee typically equal to or lower than public transit (some may be higher). Such services typically pick up and deliver nondrivers from their homes and transport them to their destinations. They need to be scheduled through telephone calls 1 to several days in advance, or they may be scheduled for routine rides such as round trip commuting to a place of employment. To receive paratransit services, nondrivers need to have eligibility forms completed by doctors or other professionals who can attest to their inability to drive or use public transportation due to temporary or permanent disabilities.

In some communities there is a debate about who can use paratransit services. For example, should an individual who is blind and capable of walking a half mile to a bus stop be eligible to ride paratransit? There is no easy answer, because some individuals who are visually impaired may be physically capable of using public transportation but are fearful for their safety and thus prefer paratransit services. Others prefer paratransit services because they provide door-to-door transportation. Nondrivers with mild to moderate disabilities may need to consider whether their disabilities justify their use of a service regardless of whether they meet criteria for using it.

Some nondrivers do not use paratransit because they perceive that there are negative connotations attached to riding such a system. They may have experienced patronizing drivers and consider other passengers to be more needy than themselves. By using a paratransit system, they believe they will be acknowledging that their disability does indeed place them in a category of people whom society views as less fortunate and devalued.

Joe

Joe, a 19-year-old receptionist, was interested in learning more about paratransit services. He had been blind since he was 5 and had learned to use mainline services in the midsized city where he lived. He was eligible for the services that would probably cut short his travel time. He reasoned that because he couldn't drive and his taxes went for roads and transit systems, he should have available door-to-door transportation.

As he was completing the form, which his mother was reading for him, she made a comment that made him stop and think. She questioned why others who did not have cars, such as those who are poor, were not eligible for this service. Joe began to wonder if he wanted to sign up for a service that was perhaps given because people felt sorry for him.

Charity transportation services are also special services. These services are provided by organizations for persons with disabilities or organizations whose public service projects include a rides program. They may provide rides to specific social activities or allow individuals with disabilities to receive a specific number of rides during each week or month. Churches or synagogues may offer rides to their functions, although their primary purpose is not associated with people with disabilities or the provision of transportation. Individual volunteers who provide rides for individuals with disabilities may also be considered a charitable transportation service, as long as no payment or reciprocation is expected. Of course, rides may be offered because someone is a friend or loved one, or even because someone wants to do a favor for an acquaintance. These impromptu rides are not always "paid for" through money or reciprocation.

Arranged rides usually are provided through contact of a third party. Nondrivers learn of a function they wish to attend. They may call the organizer of the event to ask if anyone in the club, church, or theater group is coming from their area and whether a name could be provided for a possible ride. This may be uncomfortable at first, because few organizers expect such a request. However, nondrivers can help by providing their zip code, indicating in which part of town they live, and explicitly stating the event for which they are looking for a ride and why a ride is needed. If the organizer is willing to help, it may be suggested that the organizer call a potential driver before providing a residential phone number to the nondriver. This type of arranged ride may be very helpful and a new friendship may develop. On the other hand, nondrivers may be accepting rides with strangers that may place them at some level of risk, especially if the organizer or the driver is not known to the nondriver.

Janice

When Janice moved to a new community, it was important to her that she attended temple on Friday evenings. She located two temples in the community. She called each of the temples and explained that she was new in the area and was looking for someone to carpool with on a weekly basis. The receptionist at one of the temples explained to her that if she came to services they would try to help her locate someone with whom to carpool. When she explained for a second time that she was a nondriver and was calling because she did not have a way to get to services, the receptionist was unsure of how to help her. The receptionist at another temple recommended she talk to their volunteer coordinator; together they developed a flyer introducing Janice, where she lived, and why she was seeking transportation. Three members of the congregation responded and Janice alternated riding with each of these individuals to services. She often invited the families of the drivers to dinner before services as a way to reciprocate for rides.

Advantages and Disadvantages of Specialized Methods of Travel

Specialized methods of travel have a variety of advantages for users:

- They provide door-to-door service for a reasonable cost (generally $1.50 to $5.00 per ride);
- Riders feel safe when using these services, because there are only a few other individuals riding at the same time;
- Drivers can be requested to come into the building to locate the rider so one does not have to wait outdoors in inclement weather or in an unsafe area; and
- Riders are taken to any address in a specified area.

Specialized methods of transportation also have several disadvantages including the following:

- having to preschedule rides, sometimes more than a week ahead of time
- calling to schedule a ride and being told that there are no spaces available for the desired day and time
- being put on hold for several minutes or receiving a repeated busy signal when calling to schedule a ride
- having to ride with the driver as other passengers are picked up and dropped off, thus taking significantly longer to reach a destination
- having a "window" of time in which the service will arrive and having to be ready at that time
- having to arrive prior to a scheduled appointment to ensure punctuality
- arriving late for an appointment due to other riders not being punctual, overscheduling of drivers, and so on
- having to wait for the driver to return when an appointment is over at an earlier time than expected
- being limited in the number of items (e.g., two bags from the grocery store) that can be carried on the conveyance

Loretta

Loretta decided that at 17 years old she wanted to be more independent and that she would sign up for paratransit services. Although another student who was blind told her he wouldn't be caught dead on the paratransit with all the old and disabled people, Loretta decided that getting to places cheaply was well worth it. Within a few weeks of riding paratransit, Loretta felt more independent, her parents were pleased about not having to cart her around, and her sighted friends were making comments that she was more independent than they were because they didn't have their cars yet!

Soliciting Information from Specialized Transit Operators

Users of specialized transportation systems will need to have accurate information (e.g., the address to which one wishes to travel, the main cross streets) when calling to schedule rides. Users may also make any special requests when speaking to the operator (e.g., asking the driver to come into the building, to come to the north side of the building), so that this information can be shared in the notes to the driver. Because the driver may not have received the information from the dispatcher, the user may wish to call back on the day that the ride is scheduled to review any special instructions. During travel the user of specialized transportation may wish to carry a cellular phone, so that if the driver is not there at the appointed time the user can call the dispatcher. Having a cellular phone alleviates the need to leave the pickup point to search for a pay phone and potentially miss the ride if the driver arrives during that time. For individuals who use specialized transportation services infrequently, it is a good idea to call the service the day of the ride to verify the pickup time and location.

Individuals may need to call and place a complaint if the service was not on time, if it took an unreasonable amount of time to deliver the user from the pickup location to the destination, or if the driver was unprofessional or demonstrated poor driving skills.

Kurt

Kurt was picked up from his home to go 15 blocks to a job interview that was on the other side of a highway. The route designed by the dispatcher involved going to the next town before dropping him off. Kurt realized that he could suggest a more time-efficient method for the transportation service. Politeness and an expressed mutual effort to work together to solve a problem brought excellent results. Kurt realized that different approaches to a public or business provider of transit services are in order when the problem seems to affect many persons.

Considerations When Using Specialized Methods of Travel

The process to become qualified to ride specialized transportation can be lengthy in some communities. Individuals moving to a new community may wish to obtain the paperwork ahead of time and complete and return it, so that when they arrive in the community they are registered with the specialized transportation service.

Because specialized transportation services generally provide a pickup window, the user must be prepared to be ready at the beginning of that time and wait. Users may wish to carry a book to read, a craft project, letters to write, or some other materials to occupy their time while waiting. Not only can such materials reduce the frustration of waiting, they can also be used during transit, especially if several other riders are picked up and dropped off. It is not impolite to read, listen to a book or music with an earphone, and so on, while in this form of transit.

Users of specialized transportation services are using public forms of travel and therefore must demonstrate appropriate public behaviors. Users should not engage in mannerisms, talk to themselves, or engage others in inappropriate topics of conversation. It is important for users to not converse with the driver as he or she must concentrate on driving. Users should also place their belongings, dog guide, cane, or other materials in a position that does not block aisles or take up seats needed for other passengers.

Leslie

Leslie used the paratransit service in her town to travel to her doctor's appointments, which were on the other side of town. She had learned that using paratransit made these monthly outings into a half-day event. Thus, she saved her checkbook balancing, letter writing, and other tedious tasks to do while waiting for and traveling on the van. When she arrived home each month, instead of feeling angry at how much time she had wasted waiting for her ride, she would instead feel like she had accomplished something because she had a handful of letters to put in the mail and a balanced checkbook.

Asking for and Declining Rides

Parents, spouses, friends, brothers and sisters, and close coworkers are often the ones who offer or are asked to take nondrivers home, to the store, to friends' houses, to run an errand, to attend an event, and so forth. A "dance" occurs between nondrivers and the people who are able to provide transportation. This "dance" relates to the offering of rides, the asking for rides, and the acceptance or refusal of rides. Nondrivers need to learn the following:

- how to ask for a ride
- when it is appropriate to ask for a ride
- how to work their transportation needs around others' schedules
- how to recognize when they are imposing on others
- how to recognize when they are becoming a perceived or real burden
- how to recognize when requests for rides are being refused, yet the driver is willing to consider requests in the future
- how to judge when they are overstepping their bounds (e.g., asking for a ride that is too far or too time consuming)

- how to reciprocate for a routine or frequent ride (e.g., paying, buying a meal, baby-sitting)
- how to tell when a driver truly does not want reciprocation
- how to tell when a driver is being polite by refusing reciprocation, but really would like to be acknowledged in some manner (i.e., the driver is not comfortable taking money from the nondriver, but would be comfortable with the nondriver buying them ice cream)

Asking for rides can become emotionally draining for nondrivers. First, deciding which relatives, friends, or coworkers to ask can be difficult. Also, finding the right approach or the right tone to use is important, so as not to impose on a friendship or other relationship. Some adult nondrivers determine under what circumstances they will ask for a ride in order to not be viewed as a person always in need.

Nondrivers must understand when others do or do not choose to offer a ride or agree to drive when asked. This is also part of the "dance" and nondrivers should not come to expect others to always offer rides or be willing to drive when a request is made. Reasons why drivers do not offer rides or agree to provide rides may include the following:

- having obligations to drive other people
- having an errand to run before going toward the nondriver's destination
- planning on going in another direction
- wanting some time alone
- not thinking about offering a ride even if they are going in the same direction
- going too far from the nondriver's destination
- not having time to drop off the nondriver
- feeling uncomfortable driving with a person who is not his or her spouse or significant other
- not caring to have the nondriver's company
- not having received reciprocation or appreciation for past rides

At times nondrivers will be offered a ride from someone who is considered to be an unsafe driver or one with whom nondrivers do not feel comfortable. In these cases, nondrivers will need to refuse an offered ride without offending the volunteer driver. In such situations, nondrivers can say such thing as "I don't need a ride this time, but I'd appreciate it if you'd offer again when you are going my way," or "Thank you for offering, but I've been able to make other arrangements."

Tracy

Tracy has been working with the same people for 6 months at a hardware store. Everyone knew Tracy had low vision and couldn't drive. If it was raining, one of the salespeople would offer Tracy a ride. No one else offered, even if they were passing his house. Tracy wondered if he should ask for a ride or ask if anyone wanted a job driving him to and from work in his rural community. He worried about how people would respond to either question. He was also concerned that if his coworkers said "no," then their relationships with him would change. Why did he have to be put in this position by living in such a rural area?

Activities for Nondrivers

Advantages and Disadvantages of Specialized Methods of Travel

1. (Self) Review with students the interviews of the four travelers in Section I to see what they believe are the advantages and disadvantages of specialized methods of travel.
2. (Self) Ask adolescents to make a list of all the methods of specialized transportation services. Have them list the advantages and disadvantages for each method.
3. (Others) Ask students to review interviews with adult nondrivers to learn what the interviewees believe are the advantages and disadvantages of each method of specialized transportation.

Soliciting Information from Specialized Transit Operators

1. (Self) Ask adolescents to generate a list of all the possible questions they may need to ask a paratransit operator.
2. (Self) Ask adolescents to role-play calling paratransit operators to request information about routes and schedules.
3. (Self) Ask students to complete the forms for eligibility to ride the paratransit service, including obtaining necessary documentation from the eye care specialist if signing up for the services.

4. (Others) Ask students to review interviews with adult nondrivers to learn what methods they use (e.g., time of day when scheduling may be easier, asking the operator to repeat the details of the scheduled trip) when calling to schedule transportation with paratransit operators.
5. (Community) Ask adolescents to obtain phone books from surrounding towns or other cities to determine what services are available for users of specialized services. Have them call the service providers to request information about these services.
6. (Community) Ask students to request that the paratransit service send them a packet containing the forms that must be filled out for eligibility and any additional information about the services and requirements.
7. (Community) Ask adolescents to write to several communities to receive information about their paratransit services. Ask them to compare the requirements for using the services and the services that are offered.
8. (Community) Ask adolescents to identify the committee or individual responsible for promoting and directing the paratransit service. Have them ask about the most frequent complaints made about the service and how the service is working to alleviate these problems.

Considerations When Using Specialized Methods of Travel

1. (Self) Ask students to role-play asking specialized service drivers information needed for routine or infrequent rides.
2. (Self) Ask adolescents to review the scenarios of the four travelers introduced in Section I to see what they considered in determining whether or not they would use specialized methods of travel. Ask them to discuss the advantages and disadvantages of specialized methods of travel.
3. (Self) Ask students to develop an emergency plan for if or when the specialized form of transportation does not come to the destination within the time frame given by the operator.
4. (Others) Ask adolescents to role-play experiences with people who exhibit selected inappropriate behaviors (e.g., speaking loudly, displaying annoying mannerisms) on paratransit services. Ask them to discuss the responses of other passengers and drivers.
5. (Community) Ask students to attend community meetings that address issues for users of specialized services (e.g., a citizen's advisory committee to specialized transit services).

Asking for and Declining Rides

1. (Self) Ask students to generate a list of reasons for declining a ride.
2. (Others) Ask adolescents to role-play asking for and declining rides.
3. (Others) Ask adolescents to review interviews with adult nondrivers to determine what strategies they use to ask for and decline rides.

UNIT 6—Hired Wheels: Taxis and Drivers

Taxis or hired drivers can provide options for nondrivers who have places to go.

By the end of this unit adolescents will be able to do the following:

1. Identify the advantages and disadvantages of hired methods of travel.
2. Solicit information from operators and drivers regarding transportation scheduling, costs, routes, and so on.
3. Describe considerations for nondrivers using hired methods of travel.
4. Demonstrate skills in hiring, scheduling, directing, and firing a driver.

Getting Started

Remember Jason and how he did not like to travel on his own? One time he had to take a taxi because there was no one to give him a ride. When the taxi arrived, the driver got angry at Jason when he did not go over to the cab when it pulled up. The driver told Jason to always let the dispatcher know that he is blind, so the driver can be alerted.

Think About It: What information do people who are visually impaired need to share with dispatchers and drivers? Should the driver have become annoyed with Jason?

Introduction

Hired transportation includes taxis, drivers, and rides arranged through family and friends. Money may or may not be exchanged for these hired forms of transportation. Adolescent nondrivers must understand that hiring transportation is a way of exerting independence.

Every week there are many services you hire someone to do. For example, when you go to a restaurant, you do not wait on yourself, cook the food, serve the food, and clean the dishes. Instead, the restaurant employs a variety of people—waitstaff, cooks, dishwashers—to provide these services. As a customer, you pay the bill for the meal, which is actually a payment for the variety of services and food received from the employees. Similarly, the nondriver who hires transportation is paying a fee for a service and often the use of a vehicle. There are many types of restaurants in a community and many ways to learn about them; similarly, there are many potential forms of hired transportation in the community and numerous ways to locate these services.

Taxis

Taxis are a form of hired transportation that are available in large cities as well as in many small communities. The skills required for using taxis include, but are not limited to, the following:

- hailing a taxi, locating a taxi stand, or telephoning for a taxi
- predetermining the expected charges
- seating oneself in an appropriate seat
- exhibiting appropriate behaviors
- providing a route for the driver (optional)
- reading the meter or requesting charges verbally
- calculating a tip (optional)
- understanding single or multiple rider taxi rates
- counting change
- requesting receipts

It is not necessary for nondrivers to be able to do all the skills to use a taxi; however, the more skills they can do independently and the more experiences they have, the more confidence they will gain for taxi travel. Nondrivers may not initially realize that those on business travel and vacation often use taxis and hired drivers to travel to destinations, yet when these individuals are at home they typically use their personal vehicle for travel. Nondrivers using taxis may also want to be aware of the following:

- feeling safe with an unknown driver and what to do if personal safety is threatened
- recognizing that usually there are taxi stands at airports, bus terminals, and train stations
- understanding for what services additional costs may be incurred (e.g., for additional passengers or for oversized luggage)
- giving a specific location at a building (e.g., east entrance) so that the taxi driver and nondriver are at the same location
- establishing "time pickups" for predetermined trips
- being able to locate the entrance to a building or requesting driver assistance to reach the entrance

Hailing a taxi in a congested area is a challenge even for individuals who are fully sighted. As a result, some nondrivers who are visually impaired use a special sign or button to call attention to the fact that they are hailing a taxi. The sign or button may say "taxi" in large enough letters for a driver to easily see. Holding the sign or button facing the road while standing near the curb places the individual in a position to enter the taxi when it stops. When multiple or routine rides are used, such as when travel during the workday is routine, special arrangements may be made with taxi companies for service at a reduced fee. Hired cars or limousine services are another form of taxi service. Companies send unmarked cars to transport passengers to their destinations. The rides are usually arranged in advance, along with the fees for service.

Nondrivers with visual impairments who cannot see the markings on taxis should ask the driver if the vehicle is a taxi. Nondrivers may ask, "What taxi company are you from?" as a way to verify that the vehicle is a taxi from the company called, or they may ask, "What is your cab number?" if they have asked the dispatcher what the number of the taxi will be. These types of questions are extra safety precautions that can be taken.

Hired Drivers

Nondrivers may choose to hire a driver who may be a relative, a friend, or a neighbor. Some nondrivers advertise for a driver in the newspaper, church bulletins, by placing a poster on bulletin boards around their college campus, and so forth. Some adult nondrivers hire drivers who are paid on an hourly or daily basis. Those with a sufficient amount of funds may hire chauffeurs who are available to drive them throughout the day. Although this type of driver who is at one's beck and call seems desirable, few people, with or without disabilities, have the financial resources to provide for such transportation services. Rather, nondrivers who hire a driver (other than a taxi) tend to hire someone for specific tasks such as going to work, carrying out work functions, accomplishing personal errands, or traveling to specific locations. Although getting to and from work is not usually considered a *reasonable accommodation* under the ADA or Section 504 of the Rehabilitation Act, in some instances employers will provide a driver or funds for travel to accomplish job functions.

Geraldo

Geraldo was very impressed when he saw his favorite rock star being driven around town by a chauffeur. At age 14 he knew he would not be able to drive, but he decided having a chauffeur was a pretty good substitution. Geraldo's father told him about how expensive it would be to have a full-time employee to drive all day long. Soon Geraldo decided he would only hire drivers when he needed them. His father thought this was a good idea and one that would probably work for Geraldo (who wanted to be a writer) at least until he became famous and had plenty of money!

Advantages and Disadvantages of Hired Methods of Travel

The following are some of the advantages of hired methods of travel:

- Hired drivers will provide the user with door-to-door service.
- Hired drivers can often provide information about the surroundings and location of key information (e.g., where the front door is located, the words on a sign).
- Hired drivers are efficient because they do not take any longer to reach a destination than required of a sighted person driving a personal vehicle.
- Users of hired transportation have more flexibility regarding the time of travel (e.g., they are not tied to bus schedules).
- Users of hired transportation can change their routes during travel.

Olivia

Olivia is a nondriver and a single mother of a preschooler. She often hires taxis to transport herself and her daughter. It is very important to Olivia that her daughter have the same experiences as children of parents who are drivers. Thus, she has taken her daughter via taxi through the drive through at a fast food restaurant on several occasions, an event that her daughter enjoys and looks forward to. She has hired drivers to participate in carpools to take neighborhood children to birthday parties and other events in the community.

The following are some of the disadvantages of hired methods of travel:

- Nondrivers will need to find and hire a driver.
- The cost is higher in comparison to personal methods of travel, such as walking, or public methods of travel, such as taking a bus.
- The user may be stranded if the driver does not come as scheduled.
- The hired driver may attempt to take a longer route to earn more money when he or she realizes the user can not see what roads are being traveled.
- The user may feel unsafe with the driver, especially late at night or in an unfamiliar city.
- The hired driver may not be available when the individual wishes to travel (e.g., late at night, weekends).
- If the hired driver becomes ill or has an emergency, the nondriver may be stranded.

Raul

Raul, a university professor who is a nondriver, supervises student teachers throughout his state. He has had many experiences, both positive and negative, with taxis. He flies or takes public transportation to the town in which the school he needs to visit is located, and then uses a taxi to get to his destination. Once, Raul called in his request for a taxi 2 hours before he needed it, so that when his appointment was done he would be able to leave the school and return to the airport. The taxi was not there at the appointed time, so he called the taxi company only to learn that it would be at least another 45 minutes until a taxi would be dispatched to his address. Realizing that this would make him miss his flight, Raul quickly hired a parent volunteering at the school to drive him to the airport.

Soliciting Information from Operators and Drivers

When using taxis or limousine services, nondrivers will not only need to speak with information agents to make reservations, but they will also need to speak with employees of businesses to gather information for route planning if they choose to provide a preferred route to a hired driver (see Unit 9).

Many taxi and limousine services use a time call system to reserve a ride. Users can call the day before or the morning of the day a ride is needed to reserve the ride. Some taxi companies permit drivers to accept ride reservations by passengers who call the cell phones of drivers. When calling to request a ride from a taxi or limousine service, nondrivers should do the following:

- provide the pickup address;
- provide the destination address;
- provide any specific instructions (e.g., driver should come to the west door, driver should honk the horn);
- obtain an estimate of the cost of the trip; and
- find out if credit cards are accepted or if that is the preferred method of payment.

When nondrivers enter the taxi or limousine they should do the following:

- verify with the driver their desired destination;
- tell the driver a specific route to travel if they have one they prefer; and
- ask the driver which route would be the most efficient, both timewise and costwise, if they do not have a desired route.

Nondrivers who hire drivers (e.g., a family member, neighbor, friend) also have responsibilities including the following:

- calling or speaking in person with the driver to arrange for transportation
- discussing and agreeing with the driver on such items as the payment, who is responsible for paying for the gas and tolls (if appropriate), and the route
- obtaining directions if traveling to an unfamiliar location

Eileen

Eileen works as a computer programmer for a local company. Twice a month she must attend staff meetings 20 miles away. She travels by taxi to these meetings. Through trial and error she has learned the shortest route to reach the meeting and tells the driver as they leave her office exactly which roads she wants to travel to reach her meeting. She periodically asks the driver where they are located and the cost on the meter so she can be sure that her directions are being followed. Over time she got to know two drivers and now requests one of them when she calls for her ride.

Considerations When Using Hired Methods of Travel

Hired methods of travel afford the nondriver a level of freedom not possible with other methods of travel. In exchange, these methods can be costly, so it is imperative that nondrivers use their time as efficiently as possible. Taxis and limousines charge a waiting time, so when users plan to spend a long time in a business or at an event, they may wish to schedule a drop off and then a return trip. In other instances it may be more cost efficient to have the driver wait.

When using hired drivers nondrivers must consider the following:

- Is the driver expected to function as an assistant when locations are reached (e.g., as a shopping assistant at a department store)? If so, this needs to be clearly communicated.
- Is there a place to store belongings or will it be necessary for the nondriver to take belongings when leaving the vehicle?

- Have precautions been taken in case the driver is late or breaks down (e.g., notifying the passenger by phone)?
- Have telephone numbers been exchanged in case the hired driver needs to reach the nondriver or vice-versa?

James

James is a senior in high school with low vision. He is a very busy person and finds that planning his transportation to get all the places he needs to go is time consuming. For example, on Wednesday and Friday he has swim practice before school. His dad drops him off with all of his stuff (swim bag, book bag, work clothes). He often feels self-conscious walking into the locker room of the YMCA with three big bags. From swim practice he gets a ride to school with his friend Karen. At his locker he has to take his work uniform out of his bag and try to carefully hang it up in his locker so it will not get too wrinkled. When he leaves school he takes a taxi to his job at the local hospital. He changes in the restroom before heading to the dietary department to prepare food trays. Finding a place to store his three bags was a challenge, as employers are not accustomed to employees bringing personal items to work. He had to speak to the department manager, who reluctantly agreed to let him store his bags in the department office. James resents having to carry everything he needs for the day with him from 6:00 a.m. to 6:00 p.m., when his dad picks him up from the hospital.

Hiring, Scheduling, Directing, and Firing a Driver

Nondrivers must have means of locating potential drivers as employees. For adolescents who wish to travel to local destinations, their driver may be a brother or sister, a classmate, a friend, or a neighbor. If the intention is to hire a driver, then nondrivers must be clear in their communication that they do not wish a favor and that they expect to pay for the services. Payment for the service may include the following exchanges:

- money
- baby-sitting
- tutoring
- yard work
- cooking
- buying a meal

Nondrivers may wish to hire a driver on a long-term basis. They may advertise by the following methods:

- placing ads in newspapers
- contacting senior citizens' clubs
- placing notices on bulletin boards
- asking others if they know of a potential driver

Those who intend to hire drivers for a period of time will need to obtain information pertaining to the provision of employee benefits, Social Security, workman's compensation, and so forth. Before interviewing a prospective driver, nondrivers should have made many determinations including the following:

- the extent of the driving for which the person will be hired
- the amount that they are willing to pay per hour, ride, or distance
- whether the driver will be expected to use his or her own car, or a car provided by the nondriver
- whether an additional amount will be paid for gas, tolls, and maintenance and repairs for the vehicle
- who will pay for parking, entrance fees, and so on
- who will provide the route to be taken
- whether the driver is expected to remain with the nondriver during the time he or she is at the destination
- what type of insurance the driver carries
- whether there are any chauffeur regulations or insurance issues that need clarification

Tekoa

Tekoa is a junior in college who is living on her own for the first time. Though she had been taking buses and subways on her own for several years, she quickly discovered that shopping presented a problem. It was hard to carry more than 2 or 3 days worth of food using public transportation. With her schedule at school, shopping during the week was impossible, so she decided to hire a driver. Her brother Dakovan is a senior in high school and is not doing well in trigonometry, one of Tekoa's best subjects. Tekoa and Dakovan agreed to exchange services. Each Saturday he would drive her to the stores so she could shop and do errands, and then he would come to her apartment where she would tutor him in trigonometry.

Activities for Nondrivers

Advantages and Disadvantages of Hired Methods of Travel

1. (Self) Ask adolescents to make a list of all the hired methods of travel they can think of. List the advantages and disadvantages for each method.
2. (Self) Review with students the scenarios of the four travelers in Section I to see what each one considers in determining when and how to use hired methods of travel.
3. (Others) Ask students to review interviews with adult nondrivers to learn what they believe are the advantages and disadvantages of each method of hired transportation.
4. (Others) Ask students to obtain family records of car expenses for the past year (e.g., insurance, car payment, maintenance costs, gasoline receipts) and determine the amount per month the family is paying for the car. Ask them to call the local taxi company and obtain the cost per trip from home to places the family travels (e.g., house to church, house to store, house to friend's house). Ask students to determine which method of travel (car or taxi) is more advantageous for the family.

Soliciting Information from Operators and Drivers

1. (Self) Ask adolescents to generate a list of all the possible questions to ask a dispatcher of a taxi company.
2. (Others) Ask adolescents to role-play calling taxi dispatchers to request information about routes, time pickups, costs, and so on.
3. (Others) Ask students to review interviews with adult nondrivers to learn what methods they use when calling taxi companies.
4. (Others) Ask students to role-play asking taxi drivers or hired drivers information about costs, destination distance, time, and routes.
5. (Community) Ask adolescents to call several taxi companies in the community to request costs and use these data to develop a table comparing prices. Based on the data, have them determine which company would be the least expensive to use.

Considerations When Using Hired Methods of Travel

1. (Self) Have students develop an emergency plan for if or when the taxi driver does not come to the destination within the time frame given by the operator.
2. (Self) Help adolescents learn about rules of the road and develop ways to evaluate if a driver is driving safely (e.g., if the driver "slams" on the brakes frequently this can indicate poor judgment by the driver; if the driver appears to be changing lanes constantly, this could indicate aggression, which may lead to an accident). Discuss what to do if such events occur.
3. (Others) Ask students to role-play how to respond if a taxi driver or hired driver does not come on time.
4. (Community) Ask students to call local cellular phone companies to investigate the prices and package options available for customers.

Hiring, Scheduling, Directing, and Firing a Driver

1. (Self) Review with students the scenarios of the four travelers from Section I, noting how any of these individuals used drivers. Discuss how they located drivers, what responsibilities they had, and what responsibilities the drivers had.
2. (Self) Ask students to write out a variety of advertisements for a driver (e.g., one for a church bulletin, one to hang on a college campus).
3. (Self) Ask students to generate a list of competencies a driver should have (e.g., no accidents for 3 years, punctual, willing to go into businesses to serve).
4. (Self) Ask students to review classified ads in the local newspaper to determine what wages are being offered for a variety of jobs. Based on these data, have them determine what price to pay a driver.
5. (Others) Ask students to role-play hiring, scheduling, directing, and firing a driver.
6. (Others) Ask students to review interviews with adult nondrivers to learn about strategies they used to hire, schedule, direct, and fire drivers.
7. (Community) Ask adolescents to take an assertiveness training class to refine interaction skills.

UNIT 7—Bioptic Wheels: Low Vision Driving

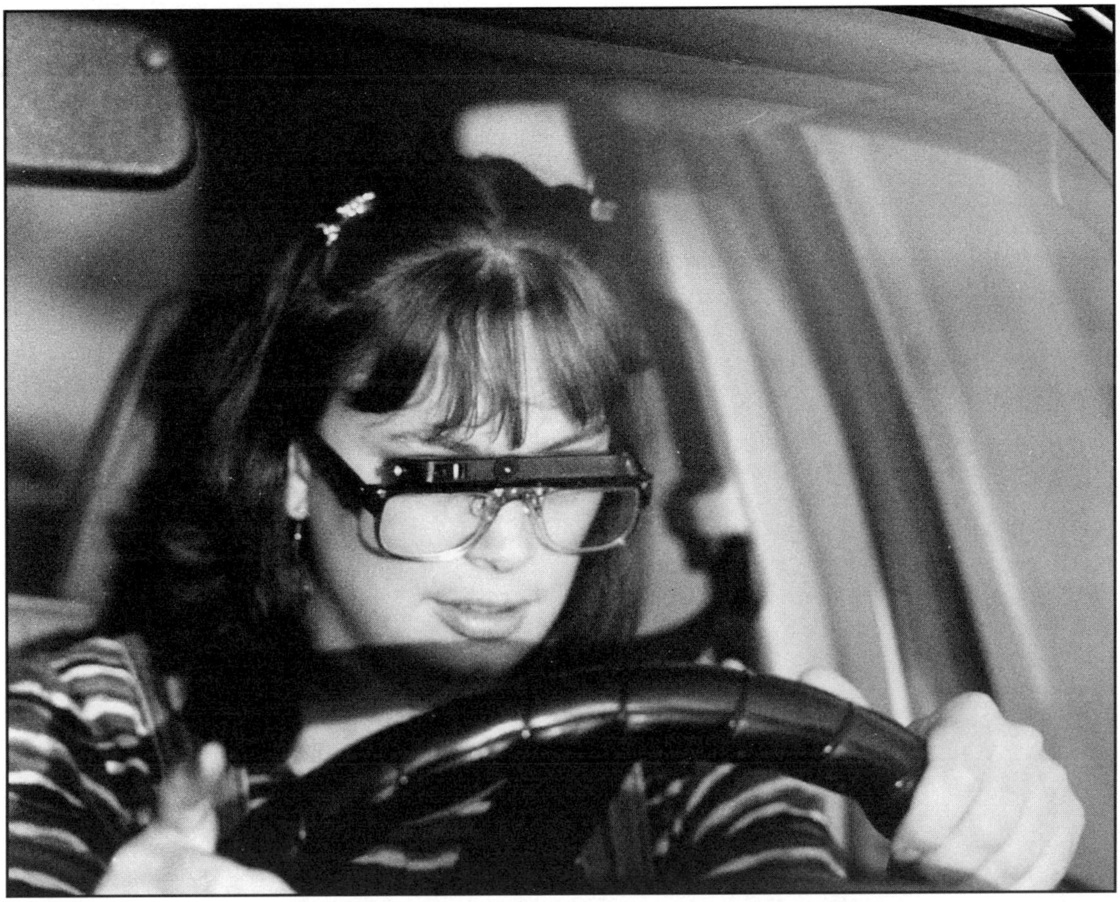

In a majority of states, adolescents with low vision who meet specified requirements may learn to drive a motor vehicle.

By the end of this unit adolescents will be able to do the following:

1. Determine whether they meet the unaided and aided visual requirements of their state (or a state in which low vision driving is permitted) to pursue driving with low vision.
2. Have knowledge of the clinical low vision evaluation that is needed to determine whether they will meet the aided visual requirements of their state (or a state in which low vision driving is permitted) to pursue driving with low vision.
3. Have knowledge of a variety of bioptic telescopic systems (BTS) and how they are used in the process of low vision driving.
4. Have an understanding of the visual skills needed for low vision driving.
5. Understand some of the differences between driving with low vision and driving with typical vision.
6. Understand some of the legal and self-imposed restrictions in driving experienced by low vision drivers.

Getting Started

Remember that when Kisha was 14 she had a clinical low vision evaluation? Although the state in which she lives does not permit people to drive with special glasses, Kisha could potentially drive in another state. Safety is the number one consideration for anyone who operates a motor vehicle, and Kisha realizes that she would have a great deal of responsibility if she learned to drive as a person with low vision.

Think About It: What are some things that a person would need to consider before deciding to operate a motor vehicle as a low vision driver using special glasses?

Introduction

Since the early 1970s, people with low vision have had the opportunity in some states to take the road test leading to a driver's license. Today a majority of the states in the United States allow low vision driving. Potential low vision drivers and their parents will have many questions. Driving with low vision continues to be a controversial subject for some professionals. Nonetheless, there are people with low vision who function very much as typical drivers in that they travel to and from work, carry passengers, and travel in an average year the same or more miles than do drivers without disabilities. For some low vision drivers the task of driving is comfortable and routine. For others it is a visually challenging task, and many low vision drivers impose driving restrictions on themselves that are even more rigorous than those imposed by their licensing agency.

Although the scope of this curriculum does not allow for extensive discussion of this topic, readers are encouraged to obtain further information from such resources as their state's Department of Safety (for motor vehicles), rehabilitation agencies, knowledgeable professionals, low vision drivers, and the professional literature on this topic. Also, the National Organization for Albinism and Hypopigmentation (NOAH) has a Web site in which information concerning low vision driving is available.

Shoshana

Shoshana always wanted to drive a car. She went through high school and college without knowing that some people with similar vision problems to hers were driving using bioptic telescopic systems. Her husband came home one day with an article in the newspaper about a new design for one of these special glasses. The article said that driving in their state was not permitted, but in a neighboring state, just three miles from where they lived, it was allowed. They decided to look into whether Shoshana could obtain a license. They would move and just commute a little farther for their jobs.

Meeting the Unaided and Aided Visual Requirements for Driving

In states that have regulations that allow for low vision driving, there are visual acuity requirements for unaided (considered with or without standard glasses or contact lenses) and aided vision. Aided vision includes the use of a bioptic telescopic system (BTS) used with the individual's standard optical corrections. A BTS includes a miniature telescope inserted into a pair of glasses that a driver uses to see details during brief viewing times. Measures of visual acuity with standard correction and the BTS are the primary determination of eligibility. In some states visual field measures and other clinical measures may be included in the visual information required before a decision is made regarding eligibility for a road test.

If adolescents' eye reports from their ophthalmologist or optometrist indicate that they meet their state's requirements for low vision driving, then a visit to a clinical low vision specialist will be their next step—that is, if their primary eye care doctor is not a low vision specialist. Some adolescents may have a visual acuity on a standard eye chart, which is close to that required for low vision driving in a state (e.g., visual acuity of 20/200 and the requirement is 20/140). These adolescents should also be seen by a clinical low vision specialist, who will measure visual acuity using special charts that pick up more subtle differences in visual acuity than the charts used by typical ophthalmologists and optometrists. These special charts are designed for people with low vision and present more symbols for different distances, thus allowing more precision in determining visual acuity measures.

Clinical Low Vision Evaluations for Driving

A clinical low vision specialist is an ophthalmologist or optometrist who has a specialty in low vision. A clinical low vision evaluation may be used for the purpose of determining whether adolescents are also able to meet the requirements for low vision driving either through standard correction or through a BTS.

It is considered a "best practice" for all adolescents with low vision to have clinical low vision evaluations throughout their school years (for optical devices providing access to near and distant information). However, one cannot assume that all adolescents with low vision will have familiarity with these evaluations. The clinical low vision specialist may also evaluate the adolescent's contrast sensitivity, visual fields, light sensitivity, binocularity, and color vision. All of these visual attributes can have a minimal to profound impact on one's ability to drive safely. For example, a person with photophobia may only need to wear prescription sunglasses along with the BTS to tolerate light conditions on bright sunny days. However, the same individual may need to be cautious about entering a highway heading west as the sun is going down directly in front of his or her face. Some of these conditions may be addressed with special lenses or approaches, whereas other conditions may reduce a person's chances for success as a safe driver regardless of whether the person meets a state's visual requirements for visual acuity and visual field.

Pamela

Pamela has *albinism* and lives in a state where people are able to drive with a BTS. When she was 15, she, her parents, and her teacher of students with visual impairments went to see Dr. Warren, a clinical low vision specialist. She was asked to read eye charts with her glasses and with several different telescopes. With one telescope she was able to accurately read the 20/40 line on the chart. Dr. Warren said a special pair of glasses that contained the telescope could be made for her and that she would then be able to see the eye chart used to test one's vision for driving. He cautioned that there is more to driving than seeing the chart, and explained that she would need extensive training in driving and how to use her new BTS in order to be a safe driver. She questioned if she would be safe even with the BTS. She also needed to consult her O&M instructor to learn about her use of distance vision in stationary and moving situations.

Bioptic Telescopic Systems and Driving

Low vision drivers use their unaided vision (with or without a standard prescription) for the majority of their driving tasks. The BTS is used for brief periods of time, primarily to confirm what is seen and not as the means through which one searches for information. A BTS is similar to a mirror in a car in that it is used for specific purposes and to provide additional information for a driver. The BTS is used for the following tasks:

- obtaining details on a sign (e.g., a milepost sign)
- anticipating changes in a road (e.g., when checking for a highway exit)
- checking for information at a greater distance (e.g., checking on a sunny day whether a light is red or green)
- following hand signals of a police officer or other person directing traffic

Just as there are different types of hand-held telescopic devices, there are different types of BTS devices for driving. They come in different sizes, powers, and with different optical properties. They may also be placed in different positions in the pair of glasses, which may include the individual's standard prescription for distance vision. Generally, a prescription for a BTS involves a telescope in only one lens; this is done to avoid some of the optical problems associated with having two telescopes. The following are three types of BTS devices:

- A BTS that has a telescopic portion placed centrally and high in the lens. To use it, the driver lowers his head and looks through the telescope.
- A BTS that consists of a lens system that is part of a rectangular segment and sits above the frames of the glasses. The user lowers her head to look through the telescope.
- A BTS that has the telescope placed centrally and in the lower portion of the lens. The user lowers his eyes and views an image that is actually in front of the user's face.

One BTS device is not necessarily better than another. When choosing a BTS, the following should be taken into consideration:

- the individual's medical condition
- the ease of use of the BTS
- the weight of the BTS on the face
- the optical properties of the BTS
- the ability of the user to use a sun filter with the BTS

A thorough conversation with the clinical low vision specialist and a chance to try these systems are necessary for the clinical low vision specialist and the individual user to make a decision about which BTS will optimize visual functioning.

Tony

Tony had always believed he would not be able to drive. He was legally blind and he had never heard of low vision people driving. When he was a sophomore in high school, all the students with low vision in his school district were sent to see Dr. Richards for a clinical low vision evaluation. Tony's parents and his special teacher went with him for the evaluation.

Tony was pleased and excited when Dr. Richards gave him a 4X monocular telescope to see the chalkboard. Tony was stunned when Dr. Richards asked him if he would be interested in driving. Dr. Richards said that when he became efficient with his monocular he could be fitted for a bioptic telescopic system for driving.

Before the evaluation, Dr. Richards had read Tony's ophthalmological report and his functional vision assessment. He called Tony's parents to discuss the possibility of driving with them. On the way home, Tony and his father had much to talk about.

Visual Skills and Low Vision Driving

Simply meeting a state's visual regulations does not mean that an adolescent should proceed with driving lessons. Low vision drivers will need to develop several abilities including, but not limited to, the following:

- becoming an efficient user of a BTS in both mechanics and when it is safe to use
- making quick decisions with visual information obtained while traveling at different speeds
- understanding road structures that may not have been previously noticed (e.g., left turn signals)
- having good use of central, middle periphery, and far periphery vision
- having good visual environmental awareness (e.g., attending to features in the environment at various distances)
- being alert to narrow (e.g., motorcycles), small (e.g., young children), unexpected (e.g., erratic drivers, road construction), or poorly identified objects (e.g., joggers wearing poorly contrasting clothing)
- tolerating visually difficult environments (e.g., sun shining in one's eyes when turning a corner)

An O&M instructor may provide assessments and instruction to prepare students for behind-the-wheel lessons with a driving instructor.

Marcus

Marcus was 15 and excited about going to see Dr. Wong, a clinical low vision specialist. He thought that he would get a special pair of glasses for driving, just like his cousin Scott, who was 18 and had *nystagmus,* the same eye condition that Marcus had. Marcus had been using an 8X monocular in school and was ready to join the ranks of low vision drivers.

Unfortunately, Dr. Wong explained that although their state allowed people with low vision to drive, Marcus couldn't meet the requirements for seeing 20/40 through a bioptic telescopic system. Marcus just knew he could be a safe driver if they'd give him a chance, especially if he only stuck to the county roads near his house. Dr. Wong realized how crushing this news was, but realized that there was little that could be comforting to a teenager who wanted to meet the visual requirements of the law.

On the way home, Marcus' parents also shared their disappointment for their son. They decided to talk with the school district's O&M instructor. Perhaps she had experienced a similar situation with other students.

Differences Between Driving with Low Vision and Typical Vision

Driving is a privilege and not a right. Driving with low vision is not the same as driving with typical vision. For example, the available reaction time for when a person sees an object may be reduced for low vision drivers. The effect of glare on a road at night and in the rain may present a far more visually demanding task for a low vision driver than for a typical driver.

People who are low vision drivers often speak of the "soul searching" that takes place before they decide to go forward with driving. Although they know that fully sighted drivers do have accidents, some of which hurt and kill children and adults, they must come to a decision whether they do in fact have sufficient vision to be a safe driver. Those who learn to drive with low vision must also have trust in their driving teachers when they are making this decision. If low vision drivers are unable to see objects, they do not know whether the object truly did not exist or whether they were just not aware of the object's existence.

Some of the possible challenges faced by drivers with low vision include the following:

- seeing other drivers in cars to anticipate their intent
- seeing hand motions of police, flag people, pedestrians, and other motorists who are signaling the low vision driver to turn or move around construction, accidents, and so on
- responding to different lighting conditions, shadows, reflections, and so on
- seeing unexpected road symbols (e.g., detour signs, lane closing signs)
- seeing left turn signals and other small details about the road conditions
- anticipating the movements of pedestrians crossing the street
- scanning the environment for the unexpected (e.g., child running into the street to chase a toy, pet in the road, intoxicated driver weaving in traffic)

It is imperative that low vision drivers understand that it is not the BTS that will make them a safe driver. Rather, it is the attainment of visual skills and the integration of visual, cognitive, motor, and other skills that will establish a level of competence. For example, if a person with low vision does not have sufficient eye-lead time and maintains attention too close to the car in which he is driving, having a BTS will not correct this unsafe problem.

Ling

After 12 hours of driving lessons with her father, Ling was still having trouble keeping her car centered in the lane and looking a distance ahead of the car. She had not ridden bicycles, played with balls, or had other similar experiences that would require her to pay attention to objects at a distance and make quick visual decisions.

Although Ling could meet the requirements for driving, her father felt she should not continue behind-the-wheel driving at that time. Ling agreed that she wasn't making progress. Driving was very important to Ling. Her school offered driver's education, so her parents requested a combination of O&M and adaptive driver's education. They realized they probably should have started with this approach. They were pleased to learn that Ling's teachers also felt it was important for her to learn to drive. At least now she'll have a better chance at learning the prerequisite skills.

Legal and Self-Imposed Restrictions

In some areas of the country, a low vision driver will automatically receive a license with restrictions. These restrictions may include the following:

- driving under 45 miles per hour
- no highway driving
- no night driving

In other areas, restrictions imposed on low vision drivers are based on observations of examiners during road tests. Some low vision drivers do not have any restrictions placed on their licenses.

Whether or not restrictions are placed on a low vision driver, it is the wise low vision driver who knows his or her own limitations. One driver may not drive on highways because she is unsure of her ability to merge into fast moving traffic. Another individual may drive at night but place a limit on going to unfamiliar areas. Still another person may have typical driving habits, but when it rains at night this person finds it difficult to tolerate glare from wet pavement and therefore does not drive in the rain. Because there may be few or many times when low vision drivers will not drive, it is important that they learn the strategies used by nondrivers. By having an expanding repertoire of strategies to find wheels, low vision drivers will be able to maintain their daily routines and independence.

Adam

Adam became a low vision driver when he was 17 years old. He's glad to be a part of the teenage culture in his school, talking about cars and about going places. For Adam daytime driving is fine, but at night he knows he just isn't safe. In fact, he was surprised not to receive a license with a nighttime restriction. Adam surely prefers summertime when it gets dark later, but he is certain to grab a ride with a friend to fall and winter football games. He always has to make a decision when he needs to travel—walk, bike, take a taxi, drive with a friend, or drive himself? He knows that driving himself is a big responsibility.

Activities for Nondrivers

Meeting the Unaided and Aided Visual Requirements for Driving

1. (Self) While adolescents are passengers in a moving vehicle, ask them to verbalize what they see. Later discuss what objects/events were seen accurately and what objects/events were missed.
2. (Others) Ask students to interview low vision drivers to learn about the process they followed to become licensed drivers in their state.
3. (Community) Ask students to contact the Department of Safety (for motor vehicles) for their state and obtain written regulations regarding driving in the state.

Clinical Low Vision Evaluations for Driving

1. (Self) Ask students to review clinical low vision evaluation reports and report whether distance devices are beneficial for them.
2. (Others) Ask adolescents to discuss with the clinician who conducts the low vision evaluation the variety of devices that can assist people with low vision in achieving the desired acuity to become low vision drivers.

Bioptic Telescopic Systems and Driving

1. (Self) Ask students to examine a variety of BTS devices and to try these on and use them within their typical environment. Discuss which devices are most useful, comfortable, and so forth.
2. (Others) Ask students to examine the BTS devices of low vision drivers. Ask them to interview these individuals to learn about how they use the devices during driving and for what other activities they choose to use the devices.
3. (Community) Ask students to obtain catalogs and other written materials from companies that manufacture BTS devices and ask them to use this information to compare the features and prices of the different devices.
4. (Community) Ask adolescents to talk with vendors from a variety of companies that manufacture BTS devices. Encourage adolescents to ask questions, try the devices, and compare features of the various devices.

Visual Skills and Low Vision Driving

1. (Self) Ask students to make a list of the visual skills that a low vision driver using a BTS would need to have. Discuss which skills they currently have achieved.
2. (Others) Ask adolescents to interview a driving school instructor who has had experience teaching individuals with low vision to drive. Have them ask the instructor about specific skills a low vision driver must develop, the sequence one undergoes during training, the success rate of low vision drivers, and so on.
3. (Others) Ask students to interview low vision drivers about what skills they have had to learn. Find out which skills were the easiest to learn and which were the most difficult.
4. (Community) Ask students to obtain resources (e.g., books, articles, Internet sources) that discuss low vision driving and the skills an individual must acquire to be successful in low vision driving.

Differences Between Driving with Low Vision and Typical Vision

1. (Self) Ask adolescents to prepare a list of beliefs about the differences between driving with typical vision and driving as a low vision individual. Discuss the differences.
2. (Others) Ask students to interview peers and adults who are typical drivers to learn what skills they believe are important for driving. Ask them to compare this information with that obtained from low vision drivers.
3. (Community) Ask students to contact the Department of Safety (for motor vehicles) to obtain a copy of the manual one uses to prepare for the driver's license test. Ask them to review what skills a driver must master in order to obtain a driver's license.

Legal and Self-Imposed Restrictions

1. (Self) Ask adolescents to prepare a list of the different environments to which low vision drivers travel. Ask them to consider the visual demands of the environments (e.g., heading east at sunrise, icy patches on roads).

2. (Others) Ask students to interview low vision drivers to learn about their self-imposed restrictions (e.g., not driving in rain, no left turns unless at a lighted intersection).

3. (Community) Ask students to contact the Department of Safety (for motor vehicles) to obtain copies of the laws and regulations pertaining to low vision driving in the state. Have them review this documentation to determine what restrictions the state has established for low vision drivers.

SECTION IV

Strategies for Independence as a Nondriver

These final three units in *Finding Wheels* give adolescents an opportunity to take the information they have learned thus far and apply it as they look at how they can be independent nondrivers. In Unit 8 budgeting for transportation and securing funding to pay for transportation are discussed in conjunction with exchanging services for transportation and reciprocating for rides from others. The concepts of gathering resources, planning efficient routes, and managing one's time are discussed in Unit 9. The final unit, Unit 10, discusses how to cope with issues associated with nondriving and managing interpersonal relationships, and ends with a discussion of public behaviors during travel.

UNIT 8—Funding Wheels: Budgeting, Funding, Exchanging, and Reciprocating

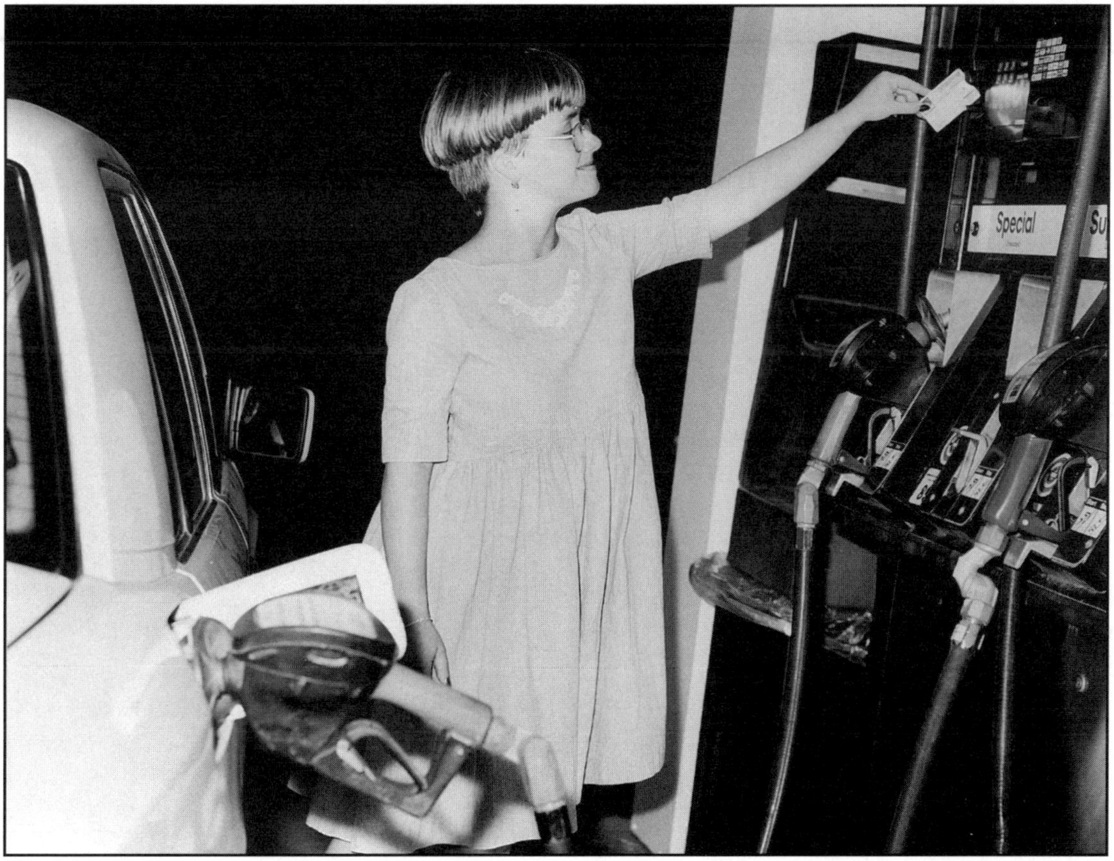

Pumping and paying for the gas is a way to reciprocate for rides that are offered.

By the end of this unit adolescents will be able to do the following:

1. List various sources of funding for transportation, including optional reduced fare programs for those with disabilities.
2. List several tasks that may be offered in exchange for rides.
3. Establish a weekly and monthly transportation budget.
4. Evaluate which forms of transportation are most appropriate to purchase in order to meet current and future needs.

Getting Started

Remember how Pablo felt when his sister told him she wished he would get an eye transplant so she wouldn't have to drive him around anymore? Pablo decided that he wouldn't feel as uncomfortable if he paid his way, so he gave his sister money for rides. Once in awhile he would buy pizza for the guys in the band who gave him rides home after practice.

Think About It: How do you feel when someone does something for you, but then makes a comment about how much extra work it is or how much of an inconvenience it is? Should Pablo's sister have been more gracious about offering rides since she had the driver's license?

Introduction

When a typical teenager is planning to obtain a driver's license, there is generally a discussion of what it will take to have one's own wheels or to borrow a car from family members. Costs of owning or borrowing a vehicle include the following:

- purchasing a car (or sharing a family car)
- paying for insurance
- paying for gas
- paying for driver's education
- paying for major repairs
- paying for routine maintenance (e.g., windshield wipers, tires, oil changes)

Because families of nondrivers often forego discussions of the costs of owning and operating a car, nondrivers do not develop a realistic sense of the costs involved. The expenses of owning and driving a car may surprise nondrivers but will help them put into perspective how costs for nondrivers compare with costs of drivers. While typical adolescents will become, to some extent, responsible for their own transportation costs (e.g. gas, bus fare), it is too often the case that nondrivers well into their adult years continue to rely on their families and school systems to provide their transportation and the costs involved.

Nondrivers may not realize the costs involved with operating a motor vehicle and may incorrectly think that there are few or no other costs other than gas. Thus, when they must spend $100 on transportation a month, they think that this is a high amount compared to someone who operates a motor vehicle. Educated consumers who are nondrivers have a realistic understanding of the costs associated with owning a car listed above. Additional costs may include the following:

- license and registration fees
- emission control checks (where applicable)
- parking fees
- bridge, tunnel, and road tolls
- emergency road services
- car washing, waxing, and other upkeep
- car rentals (while a car is in for repairs)
- traffic tickets (if received)
- parking fees

Nondrivers need to understand the costs of owning a car because they may choose to own a car and hire drivers to drive for them. They can consider the costs for drivers when developing their own budget and have something to compare their own costs against. It is important for nondrivers to understand how drivers earn money to maintain their vehicles (e.g., summer jobs, after-school jobs). Once the costs for transportation are known, nondrivers may wish to discuss with parents a similar family contribution (which might have been offered if they could drive) for transportation costs and budgeting for a period of time. Their families may also expect that in order to receive this amount, adolescent nondrivers should contribute the equivalent amount that would be needed for gas or other charges.

While some nondrivers are aware of changing gas prices and the different values of cars, they may not be aware of differences in maintenance costs or consider the cost of time when repairs are purchased.

The motivation to go places can also become motivation to become employed, to seek bartering systems, or to show a sense of responsibility. Adolescents who drive know that if they want to drive they must purchase their own gas or be the driver on the next ride with friends. Similarly, nondrivers should expect that reciprocation is part of the experience of finding and funding wheels. Reciprocation may be in the form of money, an exchange of services, or treating a friend to a meal. Nondrivers will need to place in perspective the costs for individual rides.

When adolescents with visual impairment are passive and generally inactive, they may not recognize the importance of developing independence as a nondriver. Thus, they may not have the opportunities or the motivation to tackle the challenges of nondriving.

Andrea

Andrea is a 17 year old who wants to go to the mall to purchase a gift for her mother's birthday. She feels $20 is an exorbitant amount of money to pay a taxi to travel round trip. However, she has budgeted $60 for the month for travel and she only spent $32 on getting to and from school (by bus) and hiring a driver to take her to an interview for a summer job. Thus, with $20 left in her budget she can rationalize having the luxury of taking a taxi, rather than changing buses three times and traveling almost an hour and a half to reach the mall. Taking a taxi in this instance is also more favorable than asking her mother for a ride to the mall, since the present is a surprise.

Funding for Transportation

There are many sources for transportation funding including the following:

- payment for employment in an after-school, weekend, or summer job
- allowances from parents
- money earned from a paper route or other job around the neighborhood
- money given to adolescents for birthdays and other gifts

From an early age children should have the experience of earning money and determining when to save it or spend it. Adolescents with visual impairments need to be given opportunities to earn money in the same way that these opportunities are given to peers and brothers and sisters. Opening a bank account in which to keep their earnings helps prepare nondrivers for when they will be expected to live independently and manage their own finances.

Adult nondrivers may receive the money that they allocate for transportation through a variety of methods including the following:

- employment for which they are paid
- SSI payments
- money from family members

Many cities have a *reduced fare program* for the elderly and people with disabilities. Individuals who wish to ride public or mass transit and have a disability must show verification of the disability, and then they are provided with an identification card to show the bus driver that allows them to pay a reduced fare. Using a reduced fare card may present a moral dilemma for some adolescents. They may want to discuss whether they should accept this form of public assistance. Similarly, some adolescents may question if they should be using SSI if they feel they are capable of earning their own money and do not incur additional expenses due to their disability.

Nondrivers should develop an understanding of what alternative modes of travel will cost. If at the present time adolescents only travel to and from school, their costs for travel will be at a minimal level. Nondrivers must compare what the costs are for taking a taxi, a bus, a hired driver, and other means that are available in the community. Each community will have its own "going rate" for each of these transportation methods. If adolescents are preparing their transportation budgets, these costs can be weighed against factors the following:

- amount of time for travel
- personal preferences during travel
- cost of a particular method of travel
- charges by different drivers or companies

Tyler

Sixteen-year-old Tyler really wanted to take a class on chess that was offered in town that was 12 miles away. Both of his parents worked full time and none of his friends were interested in taking lessons, so he had no one to take him to the class. He had to explore some potential methods to get there. Tyler found that a neighbor would take him for $10 round trip. He next had to figure out how he could earn $10 each week. Tom's older sister had two children and wanted to hire someone to baby-sit every other Saturday for a few hours at $4 per hour. Because she agreed to hire Tyler, he earned the money to pay for his transportation to and from chess class. After this experience, Tyler looked for an after-school job as a way to raise money to meet his expanding transportation needs.

Exchanging for Rides

Nondrivers might consider the skills or talents they possess that could be offered in exchange for rides. Although this curriculum is based on meeting transportation needs, the relationship between employability, responsibility, and ingenuity must be realized. Services adolescents can exchange for rides include the following:

- baby-sitting
- teaching someone to play a musical instrument
- pet-sitting
- tutoring peers or younger children
- cooking or baking
- yard work (e.g., mowing lawns, weeding)
- performing housekeeping chores
- teaching Braille or other compensatory skills to parents of young blind children

Adolescents must determine what to offer and how to offer the item or service in exchange for a ride. For example, would 3 hours of baby-sitting be a proper exchange for two rides to a store or for five rides to a store? Learning to be a successful negotiator not only helps nondrivers access transportation, but also teaches a useful skill needed in the business world.

Some adolescents will not be comfortable offering an exchange of services. Nondrivers should not be expected to exchange or ask for rides all the time if siblings and peers are still occasionally receiving rides from parents. However, practicing these skills is important for future success.

Adolescents must determine for themselves when accepting an occasional offered ride from a friend does not require an exchange. The extent to which rides are offered in friendship or love should not be overanalyzed with regard to proving one's independence.

Sonya

Sonya wanted to take a pottery class and her parents said it would be her birthday gift. With 2 weeks to go before classes started, Sonya had to find a way to go to the pottery studio, which was not located near a bus line. She felt her schedule was busy and although she had time for the class, she didn't have extra hours to exchange a service for rides, as she did on previous occasions.

Sonya's grandmother learned of her plight and for her birthday gave her, in addition to a wonderful present, a gift certificate for 10 rides round trip on Thursdays at 3 p.m., just when she needed to attend pottery class. Although these rides were given as a gift of love, Sonya's masterpiece from the class became a gift for her grandmother.

Budgeting for Transportation

Adolescents who have few places to go or whose transportation needs are routinely taken care of by family and friends may not find it difficult to budget for transportation. Nondrivers may not realize they have options for transportation and wrongly assume that they can only travel with family and friends. It is important for adolescent nondrivers to have the tools to make and use a transportation budget.

Budgets for adolescents and budgets for adults are the same in some ways and different in others. Similarities include the following:

- Both adolescents and adults have a set amount of money for a given time frame, such as a weekly or monthly budget.
- Both adolescents and adults must prioritize their transportation (e.g., getting to a job has more priority over getting to the mall to "hang out").

Differences in budgets include the following:

- Adults need to purchase their transportation, whereas adolescents may have school transportation provided and other transportation provided by family and friends.
- Adults will need to initiate travel to the grocery store, church or synagogue, doctor's office, and other locations; for adolescents, even those who can drive, families typically will arrange for this type of transportation.

Transportation may be a single line within an overall budget, such as $50 per month. With this budget, the nondriver determines that she will make decisions on how to travel as the need or want arises. An example of a more detailed budget is as follows:

- $20 to my friend Jane for a minimum of two round-trip rides per month on an "as wanted" basis (at mutually agreed upon times)
- $10 for travel to and from school
- $10 to purchase gas for friends who drive me to golf lessons
- $10 to use for taxis or to pay for gas for friends for other events that may arise

Prior to developing a budget, adolescents must fully understand all their transportation options and costs. For adolescents who do not yet have a job, their budget will not be complex. Expenses may include the following:

- entertainment
- lunch at school
- gas money for siblings or friends who provide rides
- clothes

Adolescents who are employed will have more money to spend but will also have more transportation costs. In addition to the costs above, they may have costs directly related to their job including the following:

- transportation to and from work
- a uniform or other items directly related to the job
- tools or other equipment to be able to do the job

Ginny

Ginny had a steady baby-sitting job on Friday nights. This supplemented the allowance her parents gave her and helped with money for transportation. Ginny decided she wanted to increase her transportation budget for next summer when she knew she and her friends would go swimming.

Ginny could crochet very well. As soon as the children went to bed on Friday nights, Ginny would crochet scarves and hats to sell for Christmas gifts. When Ginny's friend asked if she could join her family and go 300 miles to the ocean, Ginny's parents agreed to let her go and the extra $200 she earned came in handy. Although Ginny was a guest and didn't worry about transportation costs, she enjoyed treating the family to a special dinner aboard a boat.

Purchasing Transportation

Nondrivers will have to evaluate for themselves what methods of transportation they wish to purchase (e.g., bus fare, taxi fare, hiring a driver) based on availability in their communities and their lifestyle. They may believe that they are forced to spend more money on transportation than peers who operate motor vehicles. If nondrivers follow the same path as the driver to reach a destination by using alternative means, they can then get a realistic cost analysis. Nondrivers may wish to save up their errands and do them all at one time (e.g., traveling to the music store, post office, and dentist office on the same day). They may discover that it is more time and cost effective to plan days where they do their errands at one time rather than throughout the week.

Nondrivers must also consider the costs of any devices or assistance they receive due to their disability. For example, what are the costs for purchasing a white cane or optical device? For dog guide users, what are the costs of the dog's training, purchase price, food, and health care?

Another cost for travel may be money to hire an O&M instructor. Although some services may be available through a state Commission for the Blind or any other organization for persons who are blind, most employed adults will purchase this service if they want instruction in a new or unfamiliar area.

Kio

Kio, a college student from Korea, was studying psychology at an American college. He moved to a large city where he received minimal assistance from the college's services for disabled students. He contacted the local Lighthouse for the Blind and was able to purchase O&M services to learn the subway system, which was not a familiar means of travel in his rural home town in Korea. Kio enjoyed how rapidly he could travel around the city by subway.

Activities for Nondrivers

Funding for Transportation

1. (Self) Ask adolescents to make a list of all the possible sources to fund transportation. Discuss part-time jobs and how employment can provide money for transportation (see Wolffe, 1997 in References and Resources).
2. (Self) Ask students to discuss under what circumstances they would consider using a reduced fare program, if one is available in the community.
3. (Self) Ask students to complete the application process to qualify for a reduced fare program.
4. (Self) Ask adolescents to make a list for a month's time of all the activities that need to be done and those that are desired activities. For each activity, students should list all the possible transportation options and the estimated cost for each option.
5. (Others) Ask students to interview drivers to learn about their monthly transportation budgets (e.g., gas, maintenance, car payment). Ask them to compare this information with that from their interviews of nondrivers about their monthly transportation budgets. Next, they should examine the budgets of the two groups of individuals and determine who spends more money on transportation and if one group is more cost-efficient.
6. (Others) Ask adolescents to review interviews with adult nondrivers to learn how they fund their transportation and if they use reduced fare programs.
7. (Community) Ask students to contact local agencies specific for individuals with disabilities (e.g., Vocational Rehabilitation, Lighthouse for the Blind, Commission for the Blind) to request information on transportation funding if available through the agency.
8. (Community) Ask adolescents to contact the local transportation services (e.g., bus, train, subway, paratransit) to request information on reduced fare programs for individuals with disabilities.
9. (Community) Ask students to contact the long distance transportation services (e.g., bus, train, subway, paratransit) to request information on reduced fare programs for individuals with disabilities.
10. (Community) Ask students to use the library and Internet to obtain resources that discuss how to develop and stick to a budget.

Exchanging for Rides

1. (Self) Work with students to develop a list of skills they could use for exchange purposes. Discuss previous experiences with exchanging services, including those that do not involve transportation (e.g., in exchange for cleaning her sister's bedroom, Kisha was able to borrow her sister's sweater to wear to the school dance).
2. (Self) Ask students to role-play strategies to use when arranging to exchange transportation. Ask them to discuss which strategies are effective and which are not effective.
3. (Others) Ask students to review interviews with adult nondrivers to learn about exchanges they use to meet their transportation needs.
4. (Others) Ask adolescents to interview peers and family members to learn about ways they use exchanging services in their lives (not necessarily related to transportation).
5. (Others) Ask students to discuss with two or more drivers when they appreciate or expect payment or reciprocation and when they prefer to offer and provide a ride without reciprocation or payment. Ask them to compare the different drivers' responses.
6. (Community) Ask adolescents to travel to community locations where "help wanted" signs are often posted (e.g., church bulletin boards, grocery stores) and determine if people are advertising their services in exchange for services or if they are advertising for services in exchange for money.

Budgeting for Transportation

1. (Self) Ask adolescents to select a set amount of money for a designated time (e.g., $100 for the month) and develop a transportation budget based on this amount. Then have them call the transportation companies or services they will use to determine the actual costs (e.g., the cost for a monthly bus pass, the cost of a taxi from home to the mall). Ask them to compare the projected budget with the actual costs.
2. (Self) Ask students to prioritize their transportation needs and discuss with them which would be the priorities to include in budgets (e.g., travel to school, work, medical appointments) and which items would be lower priorities (e.g., travel to the mall, friends' houses). Have them develop a personal list of criteria for rating the importance of each item on the budget in order to prioritize the items objectively.
3. (Others) Ask students to obtain information about the family budget. (Some families may not wish to disclose this information.) Discuss the family budgets used in the home and obtain a copy of the budgets if available. Discuss with the family the priorities used for establishing a budget (e.g., mortgage payment and utilities are higher priorities than entertainment).
4. (Others) Ask students to review interviews with adult nondrivers to learn about their transportation budgets. If available, have them obtain copies of budgets from nondrivers and let them compare these budgets to their own.
5. (Community) Ask students to use resources (e.g., books, Internet, information from local agencies) to learn about effective strategies to employ when developing a budget for transportation.

Purchasing Transportation

1. (Self) Ask students to consider plans for the year after high school. Have them make a list of all the transportation needs they anticipate and the ways in which these needs can be met.
2. (Self) Ask adolescents to develop a preference list of transportation options to meet transportation needs. Discuss the criteria used to develop the list.
3. (Self) Review with students the scenarios of the four travelers introduced in Section I to see what criteria each uses in choosing forms of transportation.
4. (Others) Ask students to review interviews with adult nondrivers to learn about strategies these individuals use to find out about all the transportation options in a new community. Ask them to determine if the adult nondrivers considered the options before or after they moved to the community.
5. (Community) Ask adolescents to go to the library and obtain a phone book for a future community (e.g., one where a college, a trade school, or a family member is located). Using the phone book, have them determine what transportation options will be available in the new community.
6. (Community) Ask students to use catalogs, the Internet, and information from O&M instructors to learn about the different types of mobility devices (e.g.,

electronic travel aids, telescopic devices) and their associated costs.

7. (Community) Ask adolescents to contact local agencies for the visually impaired (e.g., Commission for the Blind) to find out the costs for private O&M instruction, how this service is scheduled, and how available it is.

8. (Community) Ask students to contact several dog guide schools around the country to learn about their programs (e.g., how much vision one can have, age at which one can get a dog, cost, amount of time for training).

UNIT 9—Using Wheels Efficiently: Gathering Resources, Route Planning, and Time Management

Advanced route planning can save a nondriver time and energy during his or her travels.

By the end of this unit adolescents will be able to do the following:

1. Use different resources to plan a route.
2. Create a set of directions for personal use.
3. Create a set of directions to share with others.
4. Calculate the time, distance, and cost for short and long distance trips.
5. List several activities that may be done while waiting for late rides in different environments.
6. Be assertive and solve problems concerning transportation schedules for arriving at or leaving a destination.

Getting Started

Remember how much Mary Ann wanted to ride her bike to the mall? To have more confidence and be better prepared, Mary Ann could spend some time planning her route and learning what key landmarks are along it. She could write out the directions and use a bicycle map to see where all the roads are. Then, if she does get separated from her brother, she will be better prepared to find her way on her own.

Think About It: How do you know you are ready to learn to venture into more complex unfamiliar areas (e.g., a downtown area in an unfamiliar city)?

Introduction

Although another person will physically operate the vehicle in which nondrivers will be riding, it is essential that independent nondrivers learn to plan rides and, when appropriate, create a set of directions for the driver to use. Nondrivers will need to have the skills to estimate the distance of a trip, the cost, and the time it will take to travel. Drivers may not expect nondrivers to have prepared directions or be helpful during travel along a route. However, sharing some of the responsibilities of traveling, as when friends take a long distance car ride together, is often appreciated by the driver.

For some young children with visual impairments, a car is merely a moving couch; therefore, they need to learn how cars operate and move through the environment. They may miss the incidental knowledge of what is in the environment—how roads are organized, what information is provided by signs, the function of street lights, the use of landmarks, or when turns are made to arrive at a destination.

Robert

Robert, a blind 13 year old, was with a driver who commented, "Oh, I just went through a red light." Robert's response was, "That can't happen, you can't go through a red light!" After a short discussion, the driver realized that Robert believed that a physical barrier stopped people from going "through red lights." Robert then wanted to know if roads moved or if cars moved. He had heard the phrase, "The highway is moving slowly today." Although Robert knew that cars had wheels and moved on their own, he imagined that when cars went onto the entrance ramp of a highway, they entered a moving road, similar to a moving walkway in an airport.

Children may be seated in the back seat of a car during travel. Families often assume that if children will not be driving they do not need to receive verbal descriptions of the surroundings or the logistics of how people go from place to place. Families may consider a ride without sight to be boring and so they give the children tapes or other passive activities. As a result, these children may grow up without the preparation to be an independent traveler whether using personal, public, specialized, or hired methods of travel.

Jaquin

Even though Jaquin's parents realized he would not drive, they still involved their son in planning for trips. They would discuss routes they were considering traveling and the distances and amount of time the trip would take. During the trip, Jaquin became the record keeper, keeping a running total of the amount of money spent on gas, the number of miles per gallon they were averaging, and so on. His sighted brothers enjoyed playing a license plate game, where they would each look for license plates from different states. Jaquin was the recorder, keeping a running total of which license plates each brother had spotted and which ones they still needed to find.

Using Resources To Plan a Route

Nondrivers must gather a variety of information in order to determine the most effective way to reach their desired location. When planning a route for traveling around the community to complete errands, motor vehicle drivers consider the following:

- traffic patterns
- the number of traffic lights on a given road
- the location of businesses
- the amount of traffic at the specific time of day

Nondrivers will have different types of considerations, which may include the following:

- whether a sidewalk is available on the side of the street where a bus or subway lets off passengers
- whether they will be let off on a platform or at a destination with another configuration
- the approximate length of a bus, train, or subway ride to a given destination

- whether the bus may make a distinctive turn just prior to a specific bus stop

When planning a route, nondrivers can consult a variety of sources including the following:

- city maps
- map books developed for delivery persons
- bus route maps
- city bicycle maps
- tactile maps

Some nondrivers may be deficient in their map reading skills. Some nondrivers may ask a family member, friend, or O&M instructor to draw a simplified print or tactual map of the actual area with landmarks with which they are familiar.

Information can be gathered over the telephone. Many bus information centers have detailed information about the physical features of the bus routes. For example, in some cities information agents are able to tell what corner of the intersection the bus stop is located, if the bus stop is a bench or a pole with a sign, and what businesses are located at the intersection.

Telephone directories and directory assistance may be used to gather information. Nondrivers should

- have basic information about what is found in the white pages, the business pages, the government pages, and the yellow pages of telephone directories;
- have a working knowledge of how to access long distance directory information and information for toll-free numbers;
- know how to use residential phones, pay phones, cellular phones, and credit cards to make directory assistance calls; and
- understand the cost for making directory assistance calls.

Optical devices, closed circuit televisions, and *reading machines* may be used to provide direct access to telephone directories for nondrivers who are blind or who have low vision. Telephone companies typically provide special access to directory assistance for those who cannot independently read the directory. For example, in one location a telephone subscriber who is legally blind can make up to 50 directory assistance calls each month before being charged.

Telephone directories and directory assistance can provide address information as well as the telephone number of the residence or business. Nondrivers should take the telephone number of the destination with them during travel in case they are late or need directions.

In recent years, the Internet has become an additional resource for nondrivers planning routes. Some businesses have Web pages that provide the following:

- a map of the area in which they are located
- written directions
- a picture of the building
- telephone number and address

There are also resources on the Internet to obtain maps of cities and larger geographical areas.

Cellular telephones are being carried by many adults with visual impairments. They can be used to do the following:

- check on directions
- notify a person of a change in time for arriving at a destination
- alleviate the need to find a telephone in an area when sighted assistance is not available
- provide security

Nondrivers should not count on a cellular telephone as a way to have someone "walk them through" the route of travel. Rather, it is a device to be used for the same purposes sighted individuals use one.

Joel

One of the lenses in Joel's glasses popped out of the frame. He decided to take a taxi to a mall where his parents had gone with him to purchase his glasses 2 years earlier. Now, living on his own, Joel decided not to call his parents for a ride. Had Joel considered using a telephone directory or asking a sighted roommate, he might have learned that any optician could replace the lens in the frame and that an optical store was located four blocks from his apartment.

Creating Personal Directions

To be an effective route planner, a nondriver needs to have the following:

- orientation skills
- knowledge of locations and relationships of major and secondary roadways
- map skills

- knowledge of cardinal directions
- a method for writing or recording directions

Nondrivers must be able to access the directions during transit. Access methods may include the following:

- print, Braille, or auditory directions
- print, tactile, or auditory maps
- memorized directions

Rick

Rick, an A student, rarely took notes in class and relied on his memory. He never carried a portable note taker or a slate and stylus on which to write information. One day when he went downtown to pick up tickets for an upcoming concert, he learned that a traffic problem would result in the buses on his route being cancelled.

Although he knew his way from the departure gate to the ticket area, he wasn't familiar with the routes to and from his home. A dispatcher gave the three waiting passengers directions to walk to alternative bus routes. Needing to take three turns, go through two buildings, and walk along a construction area was just too much for Rick to remember when he was flustered. He got lost twice and vowed to bring a recorder or slate and stylus with him when he traveled alone.

Creating Directions To Share with Others

Nondrivers who are planning routes for drivers will need to consider such factors as:

- time of day in which travel will take place
- time needed for each route
- errands that may be taken care of en route
- preferences of a driver to go through an area with shoppers and street lights or possibly even a reluctance to drive on highways

Taxi drivers are often more obligated to follow a route specified by the nondriver than family members or friends who are driving. When traveling with family or friends, the driver's preference for a route should be followed. However, when plans are made for a group of friends to travel a long distance, they may discuss the route together.

Nondrivers need to be aware of the types of information that are helpful to drivers including the following:

- telling the driver on an interstate highway an exit number in addition to the name of the road at an exit
- informing the driver of the necessity to get into a turn lane prior to the turn
- giving the driver a landmark to look for prior to an intersection where a turn is required

Individuals with low vision can learn to indicate what landmarks are important for the driver when approaching a destination. For example, if there is a gas station at the intersection before the McDonald's where the driver will need to turn left, upon passing the gas station the nondriver can say, "At the McDonald's coming up you will need to turn left." Although the nondriver may not see the McDonald's, it will be visible to the driver. Nondrivers must develop an understanding of "typical" distances at which vision is used for conveying directions. In addition, they must understand how many pieces of information are appropriate to convey to a driver at any one time. For example, upon entering a highway it is more helpful to a driver to know that he or she will be exiting at Exit 199, Old Hickory Boulevard, than to provide this information along with the next six directions following the exit. A discussion with the driver about the pace he or she wishes to have information conveyed is helpful before the start of a long trip.

If nondrivers use directions in Braille and the directions are constructed on a computer that provides a hard copy of Braille, making a print copy may also be helpful for the driver who wants to quickly review where he or she is going before receiving step-by-step directions.

Kelly

Kelly and his friend Sam always enjoyed fishing. Since Sam received his license, the two 18 year olds enjoyed trying out new places to fish. Kelly enjoyed talking with the men in his area to learn all the secrets for the best fishing spots all over the county. Kelly would create a Braille copy of the directions for himself and a print copy for Sam. Sam enjoyed following Kelly's directions, sometimes being surprised at their destination. On most of those days they enjoyed fish for dinner.

Calculating Time, Distance, and Cost

Most adolescents do not have a realistic understanding of transportation costs. Owners of motor vehicles have many costs in addition to gas and car payments (see Unit 8). Adolescent nondrivers benefit from talking with adult drivers and nondrivers about the costs associated with transportation. This knowledge is helpful to a nondriver in determining what is the appropriate payment for a hired driver—a rate that takes into account both the driver's skill and the wear and tear on the vehicle.

In estimating travel time, nondrivers must consider the following:

- the estimated time of travel for a personal, public, specialized, or hired method of travel
- the extra amount of time needed to arrive at a bus, train, or subway stop prior to the arrival of the transportation
- the time spent waiting for drivers who are not punctual
- delays that may occur when relying on others for transportation (e.g., the driver needs to stop and do an errand, another rider on paratransit is not ready for the pickup on time)

Trips that are expected to take from 45 minutes up to an hour by bus may require that the nondriver allow an hour and 15 minutes or more to be assured of arriving by the scheduled time. It may be frustrating for nondrivers who realize that a trip they make using public transportation may take a driver of a motor vehicle half the time or less (see Unit 10).

Often nondrivers will find that traveling a short distance can take a long time. Yet travel over longer distances tends to approximate the time this travel takes by personal motor vehicle. A reason for this is that long distance trains and buses make infrequent stops, whereas within cities or towns public transit sometimes stops at every corner. Some adult nondrivers have commented that when they travel to other cities for vacation or work, they are more comfortable taking taxis and public transportation. They rationalize that they are like other people who are visiting the city and do not have their personal motor vehicles with them.

Marcy

As a sales representative for a shoe company, Marcy travels to other cities at least once a month. Although coworkers with similar jobs often complain about the travel, Marcy feels it is so much easier on the road. Taxis are always available at airports and hotels, and quite often the owners of the stores, knowing Marcy can't rent a car, enjoy seeing her display at a hotel meeting room where she always has a catered lunch waiting for them.

Marcy figures that with this approach she has the owners' full attention and saves taxi fares equal to the lunch. Also, the owners like seeing what the competition is ordering and the owners get a free lunch. Needless to say, Marcy's sales are going very well!

Activities While Waiting for Rides

It is the nondriver's responsibility to be on time for rides. Being late can be costly in many ways. Tardiness can cost a friendship or cost the nondriver in a financial manner. If a driver arrives to volunteer a ride and he then has to wait for the nondriver, he may consider the nondriver ungrateful, inconsiderate, or one who takes advantage of others.

Drivers may be late for rides for a variety of reasons including the following:

- more traffic than anticipated
- an accident on the road
- car trouble
- having to stop to purchase gas
- getting lost in an unfamiliar area
- being inconsiderate of the nondriver

Nondrivers will need to evaluate the reason for the tardiness and determine what, if anything, they will say to the driver about the tardiness.

People who are sighted and who have to wait for rides, doctors, buses, and so on tend to carry something with them to occupy time. They may read a magazine that is available in the waiting room, or they may be friendly and strike up a conversation with another person who is waiting. However, people with visual impairments tend to wait without having a book or something to occupy time.

Cecilia

Cecilia, a woman with low vision, travels to work each day taking two buses. She has a 15-minute wait when she transfers from the first bus to the second bus at the transit center. When Cecilia first started her commute, she would just sit and wait. She found that she dreaded the bus trip because it was boring. After talking to a friend, she realized that she could be using her time better. Now she always carries stationary in her purse and uses her waiting time as a way to maintain correspondence with family and friends. She also carries a Walkman so she can listen to music or a book on tape.

Problem Solving and Assertiveness

Nondrivers who travel independently must have good problem-solving skills, because it is inevitable that things will not always go as planned. Samantha, a 21-year-old nondriver, always carries a $20 bill and at least $1 in change with her so that if she gets stuck she can call for a taxi. Ralph, a 19-year-old nondriver, keeps the telephone numbers of several family members and friends with him so that he can call for a ride if something unpredictable occurs.

Nondrivers must have skills in soliciting aid from others in the community. If a bus does not come as planned when one is waiting at an unfamiliar bus stop, it may be necessary to stop a pedestrian and verify the surroundings. When soliciting information from strangers, nondrivers will need to appear confident and self-assured so as not to appear vulnerable or unpredictable to those they approach.

Assertiveness may be necessary when drivers on public transit or paratransit are not providing the information the nondriver requests (e.g., calling out a requested stop). In these cases, using a calm, firm voice to explain why the accommodation is necessary is imperative. When appropriate, filing a complaint with the transit company may be the only way to correct the situation.

Ivan

Ivan, a 21 year old who is blind, asked a bus driver to call out the major intersections on the route. The bus driver was not willing to do this, and instead he wanted to know at what stop Ivan wanted to be let off. Ivan explained that his past experience had been that drivers on that route often forgot to let him off at his stop; therefore, if the driver called out the major intersections, Ivan would know when to ring the buzzer for his stop. The driver refused to do this, so after his bus trip Ivan called the bus company and filed a complaint. He had been sure to get the bus number and note the time of day, so that he was able to provide the bus company with information to accurately identify the driver in question. As a result of Ivan's complaint, a memo was issued to all bus drivers stating that when visually impaired passengers request them to call out the major intersections, they must adhere to these requests.

Activities for Nondrivers

Using Resources To Plan a Route

1. (Self) Ask students to identify places to travel within the community and then have them use maps to plan the most efficient way to reach their destination from a given point (e.g., home, school).
2. (Self) Make a list of the types of questions that would need to be answered when traveling to different destinations. Ask adolescents to determine the best source (e.g., telephone directory, directory assistance, calling the business) to gather the specific information.
3. (Self) Ask students to review the types of information that can be obtained from a phone directory. Have them use phone directories from several towns and cities to make comparisons.
4. (Self) Ask students to role-play calling directory assistance or a business to ask information related to locating their target location.
5. (Others) Ask adolescents to review interviews with adult nondrivers to learn about strategies they use when planning travel.
6. (Others) Ask students to interview drivers to learn what strategies and methods they use in planning routes. Students should review interviews with adult nondrivers to learn what strategies and methods they use when planning routes. Ask them to compare the differences between these two groups.
7. (Community) Ask students to contact local agencies (e.g., Department of Transportation, Parks and Recreation) to obtain maps (e.g., street maps, bike maps, walking maps).
8. (Community) Ask students to visit a local bookstore or library to determine what types of map resources are available for them to purchase or borrow.
9. (Community) Ask students to contact the local phone company to find out if a special arrangement for directory assistance is available for individuals with disabilities. Ask them to obtain the appropriate paperwork and complete this to qualify for this service if it is needed.
10. (Community) Ask adolescents to describe the different types of phone calls (e.g., direct dial, collect, third-party billing). Ask them to contact several phone companies to compare costs and services.

Creating Personal Directions

1. (Self) Ask students to determine what to include in a personal set of directions. Ask them to describe where to store these directions during travel.
2. (Self) Ask adolescents to develop a personal set of directions to a location to which they have never traveled.
3. (Others) Ask students to review interviews with adult nondrivers to learn about methods they use for devel-

oping personal sets of directions and where they store these during travel.

Creating Directions To Share with Others

1. (Self) Discuss what information is important to convey to others when giving directions. Ask students to develop a set of directions to share with others. Discuss with students the need to have these directions in an accessible format for themselves and for the driver.
2. (Self) Ask students to role-play giving directions to others.
3. (Others) Ask adolescents to review interviews with adult nondrivers to see what methods and strategies they use to effectively share directions with others.

Calculating Time, Distance, and Cost

1. (Self) Ask students to use time tables, calculators, scales on maps, and so on to determine distance (e.g., for a taxi) and the cost of short and long distance trips.
2. (Self) Ask students to compare the costs of reaching a destination through several methods of travel (e.g., taxi, bus, hired driver).
3. (Others) Ask students to review interviews with adult nondrivers to learn about ways they calculate the cost of trips.
4. (Community) Ask adolescents to obtain any needed time tables, maps, price rates, and so forth from community businesses and agencies.
5. (Community) Ask students to contact a travel agent to obtain information for planning out-of-town trips. They should use this opportunity to learn about the services offered by a travel agency (e.g., hotel booking, car rental arrangements, group tours).

Activities While Waiting for Rides

1. (Self) Ask students to develop a list of activities to do while waiting for late rides (e.g., reading a book, writing a letter, listening to a CD). Discuss where to store materials in order to have them accessible while waiting for rides.
2. (Others) Ask adolescents to review interviews with adult nondrivers to learn about what activities they do while waiting for late rides.
3. (Community) Ask students to investigate the cost of purchasing a CD or tape player by using catalogs, the Internet, or visiting stores in which these items are sold.

Problem Solving and Assertiveness

1. (Self) Discuss with students what to do if they find they are not going to arrive at a destination on time (e.g., call and let someone know they will be late, take an alternative method of travel).
2. (Self) Ask students to role-play being assertive and an effective problem solver by using a variety of scenarios (e.g., the bus does not come at the time it is scheduled and you have to get to your job interview).
3. (Others) Ask students to review interviews with adult nondrivers to learn about experiences they have had that necessitated being assertive or a problem solver.
4. (Community) Ask adolescents to enroll in an assertiveness training class or obtain books and other resources on assertiveness training.

UNIT 10—Spinning Wheels: Coping with Nondriving, Interpersonal Relationships, and Public Behaviors

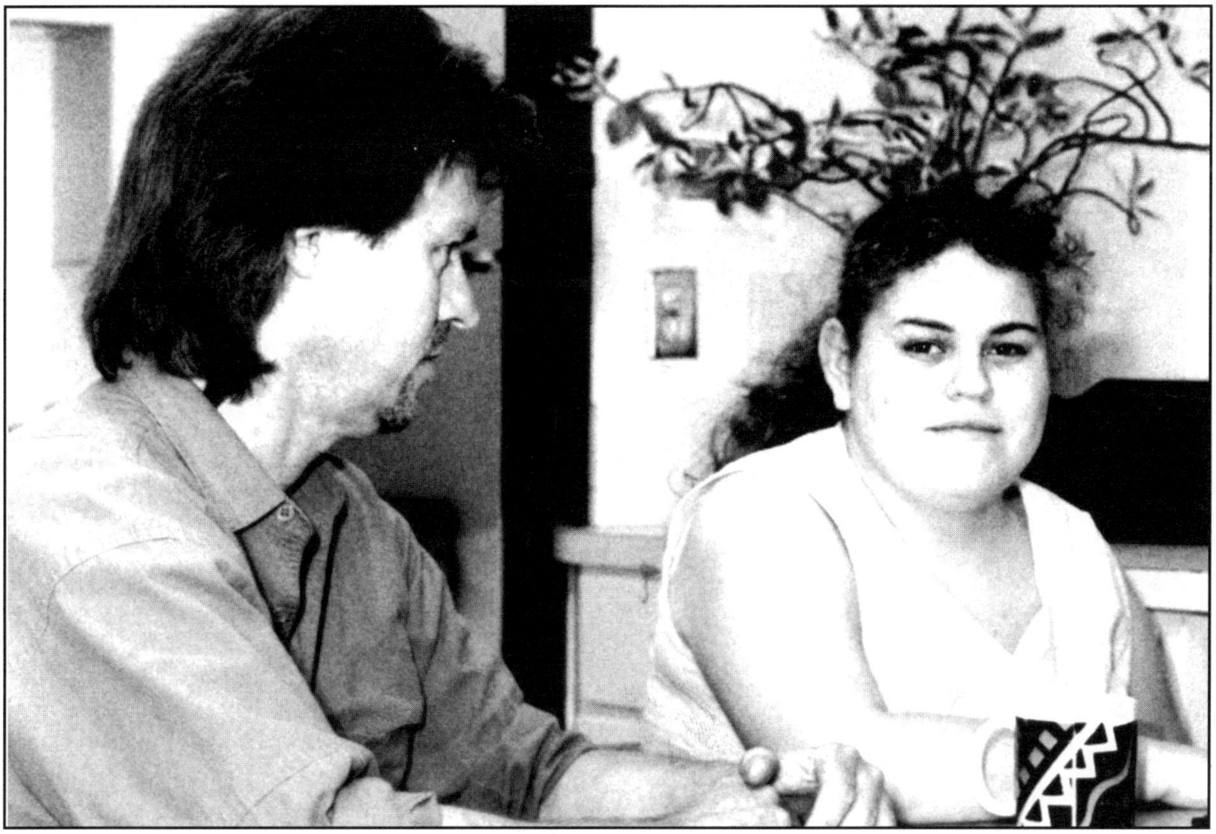

Sharing feelings can lead to identifying new strategies for nondrivers.

By the end of this unit adolescents will be able to do the following:

1. Identify personal challenges and frustrations associated with nondriving experience by adult nonrivers.
2. Provide a list of ways to reduce the frustrations associated with nondriving.
3. Identify social aspects of being a nondriver experienced by adult nondrivers.
4. Complete a self-evaluation to determine what skills they still must develop to maximize independent travel.
5. Describe acceptable public behaviors while a passenger in transit.

Getting Started

Remember how frustrated Kisha was when Mandy did not come back on time to pick her up from her music lesson? Kisha hadn't brought anything with her to do as she sat and waited and waited and waited. She ended up firing Mandy for being so irresponsible.

Think About It: How would you have handled the situation if you were left to wait for 45 minutes while your driver was at the mall hanging out?

Introduction

As stated in earlier units, as peers receive their licenses, adolescents with visual impairments experience a new loss. It is quite normal for these adolescents to feel they have missed out on a rite of passage, feel sorry for themselves, and in some situations feel quite isolated and cheated. They may begin to worry how nondriving will affect their social lives as teenagers or how they will care for their families as adults, especially if they have no adult nondriving role models. They may have conflicts with family members or friends and feel unable to stand up for themselves, when, in the next breath, they will need to ask for a ride.

Adolescents' identities may be reassessed when they begin to realize how nondriving has an impact on their lives. Their identities may take on new self-imposed attributes such as being "blind Bill" or "the kid who can't see well enough to even get a driver's license."

Relationships also change with the newfound role of becoming a nondriver. Within their families, nondriving adolescents may feel forced to rely on parents more for transportation at a time when they truly want to rely more on themselves or friends. This can place new stresses on parent–child relationships. Relationships with peers may also change as others begin driving. Adolescents with visual impairments may feel confident in participating in extracurricular activities, but be at risk of lowering their status among peers.

There have been no studies with regard to nondriving and gender differences during the adolescent years. Data from Corn and Sacks (1994) and from conversations with adolescent girls with visual impairments indicate that nondriving may have more of an impact on girls' travel than on that of boys. Parents may be more protective regarding the independent travel of visually impaired girls, especially in the evenings. Also, girls may be less assertive concerning requests for rides from peers.

Dating, marriage, and all new relationships take on new meaning when one person in the relationship cannot drive. Interpersonal exchanges such as asking for or offering rides, expecting someone to want to provide a ride, or worrying about placing a burden on one who can drive may have an impact on the relationship. Although some nondrivers can casually integrate their inability to drive into their personalities, for others nondriving takes a prominent role and seriously interferes with the development of relationships.

Jim and LaRhea

Jim and LaRhea were planning to become officially engaged in the next few months, and they were planning to marry by the end of the year. LaRhea and Jim had discussed how his not being able to drive might place some extra stress on their marriage. They spoke about how some things might go smoothly; for instance, they worked in the same company and could travel to and from work together. However, Jim was concerned that LaRhea was minimizing how having only one driver in the family might affect such decisions as where they lived and how he might want to arrange rides at times without having LaRhea be the driver. They decided to talk with another couple with only one driver. They needed to talk about this before they married so they both felt nondriving could be handled well.

Challenges and Frustrations of Adult Nondrivers

Adults who have visual impairments have identified many personal frustrations associated with nondriving. In planning for travel, nondrivers may experience frustration related to the following:

- lack of spontaneity in their life
- inability to go where and when they want to go
- having to accommodate others' schedules
- not being able to leave an event when they want to
- having a driver with them at their destination
- preplanning a means for transportation
- accepting rides that are offered out of obligation or sympathy
- carrying objects throughout the day that others can leave in cars
- not being able to run errands when in routine transit
- walking in dangerous areas to arrive at a public transit stop or destination

- explaining to others why they cannot drive (low vision)
- refusing rides that could cause discomfort (e.g., rides with individuals who drive poorly)
- feeling insecure on public transit or traveling to or from public transit
- experiencing feelings of being "disabled," patronized, or controlled when traveling with others with disabilities
- having limited choices of housing because of such needs as proximity to transportation lines and locations of grocery stores
- feeling isolated when others don't offer rides
- waiting for late rides
- feeling frustrated with others who don't offer rides
- experiencing frustration or doubt in a dating relationship
- experiencing feelings of dependency, inconvenience, and so on in a car pool
- expecting a spouse to do errands and provide rides
- experiencing frustration or embarrassment at having rides provided by parents long after the age when other adults are not relying on parents for transportation
- experiencing frustration with professionals and others who do not understand the logistics or emotional impact of nondriving
- feeling emotionally exhausted from having to plan transportation ahead of time
- arranging for return trips if arriving at a destination ahead of schedule, if an appointment time has suddenly changed, or being ready to leave within minutes of arrival

Parents may be called upon or feel the need to provide transportation long after other adolescents are independent travelers. Nondrivers may have mixed feelings about having their parents provide transportation. In one way, they appreciate the efforts of their parents, but they are also embarrassed about a continuing parental presence.

Although today men and women both drive cars, men often are "expected" to provide the transportation on a first or second date. For male nondrivers, especially those who have low vision, the need to have to explain their nondriving status is often difficult. Some adults will double date at first, allowing a friend to pick up everyone and do the driving. Once there is an understanding of the nondriver's limitations, suggesting that the young woman pick him up on the next date seems acceptable. In urban areas public transit can be used for travel while dating. In smaller cities or towns the use of drivers and taxis are options nondrivers should consider when asking someone out on a date.

Jacques

Jacques, a 19-year-old sophomore at a small college, was attracted to Gina, a woman in his biology class. For weeks he built up the nerve to ask her out on a date. Though he was confident in his personality and their ability to talk about topics of common interest, he was unsure how she would feel about dating a man who did not drive due to a visual impairment. Before asking her on the date, he planned where they would go together—a coffee shop within walking distance of the dorm where she lived. Thus, driving would not be an issue on their first date, and this greatly boosted Jacque's confidence. When he asked Gina on the date she readily accepted, and during the date she invited him to a concert and said, "And of course, I'll do the driving if you promise to bring along the CD you were telling me about for us to listen to on our way there."

Reducing the Frustrations of Nondriving

No matter how independent nondrivers are, there will be times when the frustrations of nondriving will surface. Nondrivers need to understand that it is all right to periodically be angry or frustrated because they do not drive. They must realize, however, that drivers experience frustration also. Sometimes they wish they did not drive, for example, when they have car maintenance bills to pay or when their cars break down on the way to an important meeting. Some nondrivers lose patience with drivers who tell them that they (the nondriver) should be glad they do not drive due to what nondrivers would consider a minor inconvenience.

Nondrivers have found it helpful to develop a network of people with whom they can share their frustrations in a constructive way. Family members may be good listeners and can also be helpful with transportation. Some parents will understand if their adolescents ask them to take them to a location within a short walking distance of their final destination. Other parents may be more overprotective; for example, they may insist on walking their son or daughter who is blind to the front door. Some parents may feel guilty that their child cannot drive, especially if the cause of the visual impairment is genetic or due to parental behavior.

Some nondrivers who experience frustration may find it easier to share their feelings with other nondrivers.

They may meet other nondrivers through school experiences, service organizations of and for the blind, the Internet, and summer programs for individuals with visual impairments. They may find it easier to talk to fellow nondrivers because, unlike family and friends, they live the reality of nondriving on a daily basis.

Alma

Alma, a successful self-employed nondriver, says that three to four times a year she just "loses it" when it comes to being a nondriver. The cause of her anger is often the inability to get to activities that aren't essential, like wanting to go on a hike being sponsored by a local nature group and having her ride cancel 30 minutes before the start of the hike, or missing the last bus home because she just had to stop by the vending machine for a candy bar, even though she knew that it was close to the time for the bus to arrive. At these times, she calls her sister in a neighboring state and vents her anger and frustration. Her sister understands that she does not want pity, simply someone to listen and empathize with how she is feeling.

Social Aspects of Nondriving for Adults

Adult nondrivers know that social experiences often involve a car. For example, when going on trips for pleasure or work the time spent in a car can be considerable. Some drivers will enjoy talking and others will prefer silence or music. Nondrivers and drivers need to be socially receptive to the people with whom they are traveling. There are many ways nondrivers can share in the responsibilities of trips including the following:

- paying for gas
- offering to pump gas
- bringing or buying snacks for a long trip
- borrowing a book on tape or bringing a music collection on the trip
- navigating (e.g., looking for signs reading a map)
- using a computer or other note taking device when discussing a work-related project or issue

Some nondrivers join carpools to travel to and from work or social events. Nondrivers will not be able to take their turn in driving, so they will need to pay or reciprocate for their ride. As stated previously, payment may be monetary or it could be an exchange of services such as baby-sitting for the children of the driver. Nondrivers who have children of their own may find that carpools are an effective way to transport their own children to school or social events. Again, because they are unable to take their turn at driving the children, they must find alternative ways to reciprocate. They can provide the weekly snack for the soccer team or cook dinner for the family who is driving that week.

Some adult nondrivers believe it is others' obligation to take them where they need to go; after all, it is not their fault that they have a visual impairment and cannot drive. Parents and siblings may be relied on too heavily, and thus nondrivers may become burdens and may develop unrealistic expectations for how they will meet their transportation needs. Choosing a profession such as a journalist and believing that a photographer or someone else will always be available to drive is unrealistic for those people entering this field. Nondrivers who choose to date only sighted men or women and who believe that this person could do the driving all the time for both of them may also illustrate unrealistic or inappropriate expectations.

When a driver and a nondriver are married or become life partners, stress may be placed on the relationship when expectations are not clear concerning rides and driving. When both people are planning to go to an event, the driver may always assume he or she will be driving; however, when only the nondriver needs to go somewhere, there should be an understanding of when a request for a ride is appropriate, even if the driver is available and enjoying a leisure activity. On the other hand, not asking for a ride or finding an alternative ride may be viewed as being "too independent" or as sending mixed messages about needed help. Communication is essential in any relationship. Just as couples communicate about issues around finances, leisure activities, and raising children, they also must keep open lines of communication to discuss transportation.

Joe

Joe grew up on the Navajo reservation in northern Arizona, a vast expanse of land with few towns. When his family needed to go shopping for groceries and other supplies, they drove for over an hour to reach the nearest town. Educational services for adolescents with visual impairments were not plentiful, so Joe's family sent him to the residential school for the blind in Tucson. Every 6 weeks Joe would take a 6-hour bus trip back to the reservation to see his family, and he would spend summers with them as well. By the time he was in high school, Joe found the summers to be long weeks filled with little to do. While he was at school he was able to travel by bus around Tucson, visiting the mall, friends' houses, and nearby parks to play basketball. By the time he graduated, Joe decided to remain in Tucson, where he could be more independent, even though he missed his family and the way of life on the reservation.

Self-Evaluation To Maximize Independence

As adolescents approach adulthood and realize the many aspects of being nondrivers, it becomes important for them to evaluate their own skills and needs. They must consider their

- orientation and mobility skills;
- social skills;
- financial management skills; and
- lifestyle choices.

Nondrivers should review the different modes of transportation discussed in Units 3 through 7 and rate their level of comfort and skill level for each method. Methods with which they are not comfortable or do not have adequate skills should be targeted during O&M instruction.

Social skills come into play during travel when nondrivers do the following:

- interact with people involved in providing transportation, including information agents, hired drivers, and drivers on public transit
- interact with business owners who may be unfamiliar with providing directions or other information to a visually impaired traveler
- interact with people in the community who may not realize that a visual impairment need not hamper one's independence

Nondrivers need to make lifestyle choices to maximize their independence. When selecting housing, many nondrivers prioritize the services or activities to which they want to have easy access.

Patricia

Patricia, a nondriver with low vision, has a number one priority of being able to walk to a bus stop that will provide direct service to her place of employment. Her second priority is having a grocery store within walking distance of her home or along the bus route she will be using to travel to work. Patricia's third priority is access to a library either by walking, biking, or taking a bus. When she initially searched for housing, she found only two possibilities in her budget that met her first priority. One option also met her second priority and not her third, whereas the other option did not meet either the second or third priority. Therefore, she chose the first option over the second option because it afforded her greater independence.

Acceptable Behaviors While in Transit

Nondrivers must demonstrate acceptable behaviors while in transit. What is acceptable is determined by the type of transportation being used and who else is present. When traveling in a motor vehicle with a family member, friend, or hired driver it is often not appropriate to engage in reading, listening to a CD with headphones, or other individual behaviors. Rather, it is generally appropriate to be interactive, sharing the same music, reading a book aloud or listening to a book on tape together, or engaging in conversation. When traveling on public transit, on the other hand, it is often more appropriate to do activities individually (e.g., listening to a CD with headphones on so as not to disturb other passengers). Nondrivers will need to be sensitive to the interests and needs of others with whom they are traveling, both in motor vehicles and on public transit. When in doubt about what behaviors are acceptable, nondrivers should ask trusted others.

Nondrivers should not engage in inappropriate mannerisms at any time. Behaviors such as rocking, eye poking, and hand flapping are socially inappropriate during any type of travel. These behaviors are viewed negatively by others and often are a hindrance to social interaction. Some adolescents can also benefit from information about how people sit or the directions they face on different modes of transportation, how close people stand next to each other while waiting, or how people choose seats on different conveyances.

Diane

Diane often wondered about why people seemed to move away from her when she traveled by bus. She could not see where they moved to sit, but she knew they did not leave the seat next to her to exit the bus.

One day her O&M instructor joined her on the bus and explained that when the bus is fairly empty, people leave seats empty between them to give each other space. He also commented that Diane would revert to poking her eyes when she was bored with the ride. Her O&M teacher explained that this was not appropriate behavior on a bus and made others feel uncomfortable. Together they worked on correcting this problem.

Activities for Nondrivers

Challenges and Frustrations of Adult Nondrivers

1. (Self) Ask adolescents to consider the environment in which they may live as an adult and the transportation options they will have available. Ask them to think of potential frustrations they may experience in this environment.
2. (Self) Ask adolescents to consider who to talk to and how to cope with frustration about nondriving
3. (Others) Ask students to review interviews with adult nondrivers to learn about the frustrations as well as the positive aspects of nondriving for these individuals.
4. (Community) Ask students to investigate the options for stress reduction available in the community (e.g., yoga, meditation) and obtain information on the costs, scheduling, and time commitment of these options.
5. (Community) Ask students to gather information about the different consumer organizations (e.g., American Council of the Blind, National Federation of the Blind) and the benefits of membership. Ask them to attend a meeting of at least one consumer organization.

Reducing the Frustrations of Nondriving

1. (Self) Ask adolescents to make a list of activities or tasks to reduce frustration about nondriving especially when waiting for rides that are late.
2. (Self) Ask students to role-play what to say and do when frustrated with specific issues associated with nondriving (e.g., an arranged ride that is an hour late, a paratransit driver who goes to the wrong entrance and then says the nondriver was a "no show" for the ride).
3. (Others) Ask students to interview drivers to learn about issues that frustrate them. Ask students to compare these interviews with those of adult nondrivers about issues that frustrate them.

Social Aspects of Nondriving for Adults

1. (Self) Ask students to make a list of ways to be helpful and sociable as an adult nondriver (e.g., offering to change the CD during travel, storing and retrieving written materials such as maps, pumping gas, buying snacks for the trip).
2. (Self) Ask students to think back to the last 10 places they have traveled and list these on chart paper. Ask them to indicate what social behaviors were experienced during travel to each of these locations.
3. (Others) Ask students to review interviews with adult nondrivers to learn about what they consider to be the social aspects of nondriving.

Self-Evaluation To Maximize Independence

1. (Self) Ask students to think about all the skills that have been addressed in the curriculum and ask them to evaluate their current skill level at this time. Then have them make a list of the skills that have been accomplished and those that still need to be addressed.
2. (Self) Ask adolescents to write out a plan for developing the skills still to be mastered. Identify people (e.g., parents, O&M instructor) and resources (e.g., maps, books, classes) that can help in developing these skills.

Acceptable Behaviors While in Transit

1. (Self) Ask students to critique their own behaviors and determine what may not be socially acceptable. Discuss ways in which they can monitor these behaviors.
2. (Self) Discuss with adolescents the social implications of unacceptable public behaviors and the attitudes the public will develop toward individuals exhibiting these behaviors.
3. (Others) Ask students to review interviews with adult nondrivers to learn about what they consider to be acceptable and unacceptable public behaviors while in transit.
4. Ask students to describe inappropriate behaviors of other nondrivers that they have encountered.

Final Thoughts

Now that you and the adolescents have made it through the *Finding Wheels* curriculum, we hope that the adolescents have grown through this experience and have learned new skills. Most importantly, we hope adolescents have developed strategies to take control of their transportation needs and have begun to think about whether they will choose independent and active lifestyles. We hope you will share your experiences with *Finding Wheels* with us and suggest additional strategies that could be added. We look forward to hearing from you and from the adolescents with whom you have worked. We thank you for your time and your willingness to help us further develop the best curriculum possible on this topic.

Dr. Anne L. Corn
Peabody College of Vanderbilt University
P.O. Box 328
Nashville, TN 37203
615/322-2249
Anne.Corn@Vanderbilt.edu
or
Dr. L. Penny Rosenblum
Department of Special Education, Rehabilitation, and School Psychology
University of Arizona
P.O. Box 210069
Tucson, AZ 85721-0069
520/621-7822

Glossary

albinism reduced pigment in the iris, choroid, and possibly the hair and skin. Individuals with albinism typically have reduced acuity, sensitivity to light (photophobia), and often nystagmus (rapid eye movement).

Americans with Disability Act (ADA) a law passed by Congress in 1990 with multiple purposes, including providing access to public transportation for individuals with disabilities.

bioptic telescopic system (BTS) a miniature telescope mounted into a person's regular glasses, positioned above or below the direct line of sight when facing forward. The BTS is used for distance vision and in many states enables some individuals with low vision to obtain an acuity for driving purposes.

cataracts an opacity or clouding of the lens resulting in reduced visual acuity and photophobia.

cerebral palsy (CP) a disorder of movement resulting from damage to the brain during prenatal development to approximately 8 to 12 years. Cerebral palsy affects muscle control.

charity transportation services arranged transportation often through an agency or group for people with disabilities, a church, or a community volunteer service. Riders must meet a specified criteria (e.g., disabled, elderly).

clinical low vision specialists an ophthalmologist or optometrist with a specialty in the care of children and adults with low vision.

closed circuit television (CCTV) a device that provides electronic magnification by means of a video camera that projects the image onto a television monitor.

color vision the perception of color as a result of the stimulation of specialized cone receptors in the retina.

contrast sensitivity the ability to detect differences in grayness and background.

glaucoma a disease in which increased intraocular pressure results in the degeneration of the optic disk and eventual defects in the visual field.

Individuals with Disabilities Education Act (IDEA) a federal law that provides a free, appropriate public education for adolescents with disabilities including visual impairment. Under this law, adolescents with visual impairment with documented needs receive instruction from a teacher of children with visual impairment and an O&M instructor.

legally blind a visual impairment in which distance visual acuity is 20/200 or less in the better eye with best correction with conventional lenses, or visual field restriction of 20 degrees or less in the better eye with best correction. Legal blindness is often used as a criteria for determining eligibility for services in the United States.

low vision a visual impairment after correction, but with the potential for use of available vision with or without optical or nonoptical compensatory visual strategies, devices, and environmental modifications, to plan and perform daily tasks.

mainline transportation a city's or town's transportation for its citizens; may include such conveyances as buses and trains.

mass transportation methods of people moving in large cities in order to avoid congestion on roadways.

monocular telescope a telescope that can be used with one eye for distance viewing.

nystagmus an involuntary oscillation (movement) of the eye that may be horizontal, vertical, and/or pendular.

optical devices any system of lenses that enhances visual functioning (e.g., magnifying glass, stand magnifier, monocular telescope, BTS).

ophthalmologist a physician who specializes in the treatment of defects and diseases of the eyes, performs surgery when necessary, and prescribes other types of treatment including eyeglasses, contact lenses, medications, and optical devices.

orientation and mobility instructor a professional who specializes in teaching travel skills to visually impaired people, including the use of a cane, dog guide, or sophisticated electronic travel aid as well as the sighted guide technique.

paratransit services door-to-door transportation in accessible vehicles, restricted to individuals with disabilities or elderly persons.

public transportation transportation for those who cannot or choose not to drive for various reasons including disability, affordability, and age.

reading machine a machine that scans print and reads it out in speech or saves it to a computer disk.

reasonable accommodation an accommodation that is needed for an individual to have access to the same service as those people without disabilities (e.g., free use of directory assistance for someone who is blind so that the individual can access the print phone book.

reduced fare program a program through which an individual qualifies for a lower fare because he or she has a disability or is elderly.

retinolblastoma a malignant tumor in the eye that develops in early childhood.

retinopathy of prematurity (ROP) a common cause of visual impairment in premature infants.

Section 504 of the Rehabilitation Act provides individuals with disabilities protection against discrimination in any program that is federally funded.

seizure disorder (epilepsy) a neurological disorder in which normal brain activity is disrupted by excessive electrical discharge. Some individuals have tonic-clonic (grand mal) seizures, which are severe, whereas others have mild seizures known as absence (petit mal).

Supplemental Social Security Income (SSI) available to those who are legally blind and who do not work due to their disability.

visual acuity the sharpness of vision with respect to the ability to distinguish detail, often measured as the eye's ability to distinguish the details and shapes of objects at a designated distance.

visual field the area that can be seen when looking straight ahead, measured in degrees from the fixation point.

References and Resources

References and Recommended Readings

Ambrose, G. V., & Corn, A. L. (1997). Impact of low vision on orientation. *Re:view, 19*, 80–96.

Blasch, B. B., Wiener, W. R., & Welsh, R. L. (1997). *Foundations of orientation and mobility* (2nd ed.). New York: American Foundation for the Blind.

Corn, A. L., & Koenig, A. J. (1996). *Foundations of low vision: Clinical and functional perspectives*. New York: American Foundation for the Blind.

Corn, A. L., & Sacks, S. Z. (1994). The impact of nondriving on adults with visual impairments. *Journal of Visual Impairment and Blindness*, 88(1), 53–68.

Golledge, R. G., Marston, J. R., & Costanzo, C. M. (1997). Attitudes of visually impaired persons toward the use of public transportation. *Journal of Visual Impairment and Blindness, 91*(5), 446–459.

Jacobson, B. (1993). *The art and science of teaching orientation and mobility to persons with visual impairments*. New York: American Foundation for the Blind.

Kirchner, C., McBroom, L. W., Nelson, K. A., & Graves, W. H. (1992). *Lifestyles of employed legally blind people: A study of expenditures and time use (final report)*. Starkville: Mississippi State University, Rehabilitation Research and Training Center on Blindness and Low Vision.

Laus, M. (1977). *Travel instruction for the handicapped*. Springfield, IL: Charles C. Thomas.

Pava, W. S. (1991). Visually impaired persons' vulnerability to sexual and physical assault. *Journal of Visual Impairment and Blindness*, 88(2), 103–112.

Pava, W. S., Bateman, M. K., & Glascock, A. J. (1991). Self-defense training for visually impaired women. *Journal of Visual Impairment and Blindness*, 85(10), 397–401.

Sacks, S. Z., & Corn, A. L. (1990). Adolescents with visual impairments: Do they understand their disability? *Journal of Visual Impairment and Blindness*, 90(5), 412–422.

Sauerberger, D. (1993). *Independence without sight or sound: Suggestions for practitioners working with deaf-blind adults*. New York: American Foundation for the Blind.

Uslan, M. M., Peck, A. F., Wiener, W. R., & Stern, A. (1990). *Access to mass transit for blind and visually impaired travelers*. New York: American Foundation for the Blind.

Wolffe, K. (Ed.). (1999). *Skills for success: A career education handbook for children and adolescents with visual impairment*. New York: American Foundation for the Blind.

Wolffe, K., & Sacks, S. Z. (1997). The lifestyles of blind, low vision, and sighted youths: A quantitative comparison. *Journal of Visual Impairment and Blindness, 91*(3), 245–257.

Recommended Curriculums

Loumiet, R., & Levack, N. (1993). *Independent living: A curriculum with adaptations for adolescents with visual impairments* (2nd ed.). Austin: Texas School for the Blind and Visually Impaired.

Pogrund, R., Healy, G., Jones, K., Levack, N., Martin-Curry, S., Martinez, C., Marz, J., Roberson-Smith, B., & Vrba, A. (1993). *TAPS: An orientation and mobility curriculum for adolescents with visual impairments*. Austin: Texas School for the Blind and Visually Impaired.

Wolffe, K. (1997). *Transition tote system: Navigating the rapids of life*. Louisville, KY: American Printing House for the Blind.

Sources for Maps

Local book stores will be a good source for finding standard maps and maps that are designed with enlarged sections of cities and towns. There are also books such as *The Exit Authority* (available from Interstate America Publishing) that provide information about interstate highway exits. Tactile maps may be obtained from the American Printing House for the Blind, P. O. Box 6085, 1839 Frankfort Ave., Louisville, Kentucky 40206-0085.